ANGLO-EUROPEAN COLLEGE OF CE

ICSS

INTERNATIONAL CONGRESS AND SYMPOSIUM SERIES 212

Editor-in-Chief Lord Walton of Detchant

Evaluating clinical audit:
past lessons, future directions

Edited by
Kieran Walshe

Proceedings of a conference organized by the Royal Society of Medicine and CASPE Research with the support of the Department of Health, held in London on 27 April, 1995

The ROYAL
SOCIETY *of*
MEDICINE
PRESS *Limited*

These proceedings are published by Royal Society of Medicine Services Ltd with financial support from the sponsor. The contributors are responsible for the scientific content and for the views expressed, which are not necessarily those of the sponsor, of the editor of the series or of the volume, of the Royal Society of Medicine or of the Royal Society of Medicine Press Ltd. Distribution has been in accordance with the wishes of the sponsor but a copy is available to any Fellow of the Society at a privileged price.

British Library Cataloguing in Publication Data
A catalogue record for this book is available from the British Library
ISBN 1-85315-270-6
ISSN 0142-2367

Phototypeset by Dobbie Typesetting Limited, Tavistock, Devon
Printed in Great Britain by Ebenezer Baylis, The Trinity Press, Worcester

Contributors

James Coles

DIRECTOR OF CASPE RESEARCH, 76 BOROUGH HIGH STREET, LONDON SE1 1LL, UK

Gill Harvey

RCN SENIOR RESEARCH AND DEVELOPMENT OFFICER, THE NATIONAL INSTITUTE FOR NURSING,
RADCLIFFE INFIRMARY, WOODSTOCK ROAD, OXFORD OX2 6HE, UK

Alison Kitson

DIRECTOR OF THE NATIONAL INSTITUTE FOR NURSING,
RADCLIFFE INFIRMARY, WOODSTOCK ROAD, OXFORD OX2 6HE, UK

Peter Littlejohns

DIRECTOR OF THE HEALTH CARE EVALUATION UNIT, DEPARTMENT OF PUBLIC HEALTH SCIENCES,
ST GEORGE'S HOSPITAL MEDICAL SCHOOL, CRANMER TERRACE, TOOTING, LONDON SW17 0RE, UK

Joanne Lord

RESEARCH FELLOW, THE HEALTH CARE EVALUATION UNIT, DEPARTMENT OF PUBLIC HEALTH SCIENCES,
ST GEORGE'S HOSPITAL MEDICAL SCHOOL, CRANMER TERRACE, TOOTING, LONDON SW17 0RE, UK

Clare Morrell

RCN CLINICAL AUDIT DEVELOPMENT OFFICER AT THE NATIONAL INSTITUTE FOR NURSING,
RADCLIFFE INFIRMARY, WOODSTOCK ROAD, OXFORD OX2 6HE, UK

Tim Packwood

SENIOR LECTURER, DEPARTMENT OF GOVERNMENT, BRUNEL UNIVERSITY,
UXBRIDGE, MIDDLESEX UB8 3PH, UK

Brian Payne

DIRECTOR (HEALTH), THE NATIONAL AUDIT OFFICE, BUCKINGHAM PALACE ROAD,
LONDON SW1W 9SP, UK

Kieran Walshe

SENIOR RESEARCH FELLOW, THE HEALTH SERVICES MANAGEMENT CENTRE,
UNIVERSITY OF BIRMINGHAM, PARK HOUSE, 40 EDGBASTON PARK ROAD, BIRMINGHAM B15 2RT, UK

Contents

ANGLO-EUROPEAN COLLEGE OF CHIROPRACTIC

Introduction

In 1989, the UK government introduced a mandatory form of quality assurance in healthcare for the first time in the history of the NHS. In the White Paper[1] published in January of that year and in later health circulars, the Department of Health required all doctors[2] and subsequently encouraged many other health professionals[3] to take part in clinical audit. Although this sounds a rather dramatic and potentially controversial course of action, in reality it provoked little protest or opposition, for three reasons. Firstly, this reform was part of a package of measures, some of which were more obviously contentious. These other measures, like the creation of NHS trusts and the development of the internal market, drew the fire that might otherwise have been directed at audit. Secondly, the government's approach to implementing this reform was marked by a desire not to upset professional sensitivities and was consequently largely non-directive. The nature of clinical audit, the mechanisms for making it work, the structures and systems needed—all were left in the hands of the clinicians, primarily senior medical staff, who were given control of the resources specially allocated to setting up audit. Thirdly, audit was well resourced, through a total central investment of over £220 million in England between 1989 and 1994. These ringfenced funds attracted the interest and softened the opposition of many clinicians.

Like the other reforms introduced in 1989, clinical audit was a largely untested innovation, and an unknown quantity. Its impact on the NHS could only be guessed at, and no-one really knew how effective it would be in creating systems for measuring and improving the quality of care in the NHS. Although quality assurance and clinical audit had long been features of healthcare systems in other countries, the evidence for the effectiveness of such programmes was generally weak and incomplete[4]. Again, though some formal audit activities and quality measurement had taken place in the NHS for many years, in particular specialties or through the enthusiasm of particular individuals, there was little evidence that the results really justified the investment. In this light, the Department of Health's decision to support the development of clinical audit and to invest so heavily in it might be readily questioned and challenged.

EVALUATING CLINICAL AUDIT: PAST LESSONS, FUTURE DIRECTIONS, EDITED BY KIERAN WALSHE, 1995.
INTERNATIONAL CONGRESS AND SYMPOSIUM SERIES NO 212 PUBLISHED BY ROYAL SOCIETY OF MEDICINE PRESS LIMITED

Evaluation was not initially a popular concept with the originators of the NHS reforms[5], but it is to the Department of Health's credit that between 1990 and 1995 a number of evaluations of the development of clinical audit and its impact on the quality of care were initiated by the Department and other agencies[6]. CASPE Research, an independent research unit linked to the King's Fund was commissioned to undertake evaluation work on the medical, nursing and therapy and clinical audit programmes. Brunel University and King's College London were funded to evaluate the development of audit in the therapy professions, and Brunel also undertook work on medical audit with the support of the King's Fund. The Health Care Evaluation Unit at St George's Hospital was commissioned to evaluate the development of audit in relation to purchasing, and the Health Services Research Unit at the London School of Hygiene (in cooperation with other partners) was funded to examine the cost-effectiveness of audit. The National Institute for Nursing in Oxford was commissioned to undertake work on the development of nursing audit and particularly on the impact of DySSSy standard-setting approach. Researchers at the Royal Free Hospital and separately at the Eli Lilly Clinical Audit Centre in Leicester were funded to evaluate the development of audit in primary care. At the same time, the National Audit Office, which is independent of government and reports directly to Parliament on the effectiveness, efficiency and economy with which public funds have been used, set up its own evaluation of the audit programmes in England, Wales and Scotland.

Together, these studies make up a substantial body of research into the implementation of audit and quality improvement programmes in healthcare and their impact on healthcare organizations and on the quality of care for patients. The development of clinical audit in the NHS has now been quite thoroughly and extensively studied. The findings of this work should be of value to all those with an interest in the quality of care in the NHS, and the lessons it teaches should also be of help to those from other countries, in Europe and elsewhere, who are engaged in setting up audit and quality improvement programmes.

For the NHS, the results of these various evaluations arrive at an apposite moment. The task of moving forward on clinical audit has ceased to be centrally driven by the Department of Health, and has become a local issue for purchasers and providers to agree between themselves. The funds for clinical audit activities have been incorporated into health authorities' general financial allocations. Five years of generous funding and considerable freedom of action for those involved in clinical audit have passed. Additionally, many new issues and problems crowd the agenda for clinicians and managers alike, as the pace of organizational change within the NHS continues and new policy initiatives, like the growing emphasis on evidence-based practice, take shape. Amid a raft of other pressing priorities and new ideas, clinical audit may find it harder to demand clinicians' and managers' attention in future. For all these reasons, it is time for those with an interest in clinical audit to pause, take stock, and think carefully about its future.

At the Royal Society of Medicine in April 1995, we brought together researchers who had been working on some of these different evaluations of audit and quality improvement programmes, for a meeting entitled *Evaluating clinical audit: past lessons, future directions*. This conference was intended to provide the first opportunity to hear about the results of several separate evaluation initiatives in a single forum. The aim was to begin to understand what they, both jointly and individually, tell us about the progress that has been made in establishing clinical audit within the NHS and the impact that audit has had on the quality of care. This publication is intended to serve the same purpose, but for a wider audience. While the reader can always consult the published reports and journal papers from each of the five studies described here, this publication is intended to provide an overview of the key messages and findings from each project.

We are indebted to those involved in the research studies reported here, who made time both to present at the conference and to write papers for this publication. We would also like to thank Dr Charles Shaw and Dr Fiona Moss who chaired the conference, those who took part in two panel discussions which are not reported here, all those who attended the conference, and the Department of Health who part funded the meeting. Finally, thanks are due to the RSM Forum on Quality in Healthcare, which hosted the conference, and particularly to the Forums Office staff for all their help with its administration.

Kieran Walshe

James Coles

References

1   Department of Health. *Working for patients*. London: HMSO, 1989

2   Department of Health. HC(91)2. *Medical audit in the Hospital and Community Health Services*. London: Department of Health, 1991

3   Department of Health. *The evolution of clinical audit*. London: Department of Health, 1993

4   Walshe K, Coles J. *Evaluating audit: developing a framework*. London: CASPE Research, 1993

5   Robinson R, Le Grand J. *Evaluating the NHS Reforms*. London: King's Fund Institute, 1994

6   Walshe K, Coles J. *Evaluating audit: a review of initiatives*. London: CASPE Research, 1993

Clinical audit: is it value for money?

BRIAN PAYNE

THE NATIONAL AUDIT OFFICE, LONDON, UK

This paper explains why the National Audit Office decided to examine the Government's initiative on clinical audit and describes the main findings of the National Audit Office report on *Auditing clinical care in Scotland* [1]. It goes on to outline the Committee of Public Accounts' views on the clinical audit initiative based on this report and their examination of the Chief Executive of the NHS in Scotland, and the Government's response to the Committee's recommendations. Finally, in the light of these reports, it considers if it is possible to come to any conclusions about whether a national initiative to introduce clinical audit represents good value for money.

The National Audit Office

The role of the National Audit Office (NAO) is to provide information and advice to Parliament on the way government departments and many other public bodies account for and use taxpayers' money. The NAO is independent of Government and is not part of the Civil Service or the NHS.

There are two aspects to the work of the NAO, financial audit and value for money audit. On the financial side, the Comptroller and Auditor General, the head of the NAO, is responsible for certifying the accounts of government departments and other public bodies. The Comptroller and Auditor General is also empowered to look at the economy, efficiency and effectiveness of any area of Government expenditure. The main way in which this task is

EVALUATING CLINICAL AUDIT: PAST LESSONS, FUTURE DIRECTIONS, EDITED BY KIERAN WALSHE, 1995.
INTERNATIONAL CONGRESS AND SYMPOSIUM SERIES NO 212 PUBLISHED BY ROYAL SOCIETY OF MEDICINE PRESS LIMITED

carried out is through publication of value for money reports to Parliament, such as the report on Auditing Clinical Care in Scotland.

The selection of clinical audit for examination

In 1989 the White Paper *Working for Patients*[2] was published; it announced the introduction of better audit arrangements including clinical audit. The development of systematic clinical audit was, therefore, one of the major themes of the Government's reform of the NHS, and it has the potential to have a major impact on the quality of care provided for patients in the NHS. For these reasons it was decided that this was a subject which was appropriate for an examination by the NAO and a report to Parliament.

Clinical audit has developed in slightly different ways, and at a different pace in Scotland, England and Wales. The NAO decided to look at how the initiative had been introduced in Scotland first. The report on Scotland was published in March 1994. The NAO has also examined progress in England.

The examination of clinical audit in Scotland concentrated on two major aspects; the impact so far of auditing clinical care, and the measures being taken to develop clinical audit. The NAO visited five health boards in Scotland and a selection of provider units, NHS trusts and general practices. The medical Royal Colleges and the Scottish Office were also consulted.

There is no complete consensus over the use of various terms to describe the audit of clinical care. For the purposes of this paper clinical audit is used as a generic term encompassing uni-professional and multi-professional audit.

Findings

Although the NAO examined the initiative at an early stage of its introduction, they found that the Scottish Office's investment was contributing to changes in clinical practice, organization and management which were leading to improvements in patient care. A number of examples were described in the report including audits of wound infections, treatment of asthma, pathology support in thyroid surgery and administration of drugs.

The Government's objective was that all health professionals should take part in audit. At the time the NAO looked at the development of clinical audit they concluded that while not all health professionals were involved in audit yet, substantial progress had been made towards that goal. About 60% of the specialties in Scotland were participating in audit, and about 50% of general practitioners were involved in audit projects.

They also found at the hospitals visited that more activity was going on which was not funded from central ringfenced audit resources than that which was. The system of audit had been professionally led, as it was intended to be, and there had been no problems with maintaining the confidentiality of audit results in respect of individual patients.

There were, however, a number of constraints, in particular a shortage of time on the part of health professionals to undertake audit, the need for adequate numbers of support staff to enable doctors, nurses and other health professionals to audit, and problems created by the lack of good quality clinical information systems which could be easily accessed. There were also a number of problems with the financial management of audit funds, leading to delays in allocations being notified to hospitals and, at that stage, a degree of uncertainty over funding arrangements at local level as the Scottish Office moved away from specific ringfenced monies to including allocations for audit within the overall general allocation. There were also some concerns which were expressed to the NAO by many of the clinicians concerned. In particular, the concerns were about the future involvement of non-clinicians, of managers mainly, in setting priorities and in making decisions about the funding for audit.

The Scottish Office had recognized these issues and had already moved to address these concerns. One of the results was the report of a committee chaired by Sir Thomas Thomson, Chairman of the Greater Glasgow Health Board on *The interface between clinical audit and management*[3]. Amongst other things the report suggested criteria for undertaking an audit. There were:

— the issue addressed is a common problem;

— it is a significant or serious problem;

— change following audit is likely to benefit patients;

— change is likely to lead to greater effectiveness;

— the issue is relevant to professional practice or development;

— there is a realistic potential for improvement;

— the end result is likely to justify the investment of time and effort involved.

These criteria were an attempt to assess the costs and benefits, or value for money, of individual audit projects. Although some elements are judgmental, the basic assumption underlying the application of these criteria is that resources should only be made available to support those clinical audit projects where, on the face of it, the benefits were likely to justify the costs.

The Report of the Committee of Public Accounts

The NAO report was considered by the Committee of Public Accounts (the PAC) at a hearing on 27 April 1994. The PAC is a cross party select committee of some 15 MPs under the chairmanship of the Rt Hon Robert Sheldon MP. The PAC examine the Accounting Officer, who in this case was Mr Geoff Scaife, the Chief Executive of the NHS in Scotland. The hearing was based on the NAO report and lasted about two to three hours. The PAC produced a report which was published on 2 November 1994[4] based on their findings and making recommendations for further Government action.

There were three main issues which were of interest to the PAC: the level of participation in clinical audit by health professionals; how costs and benefits were being evaluated; and whether clinical audit was being integrated into the management structure of the NHS in Scotland.

The PAC concluded that the level of participation by health professionals in clinical audit in Scotland was rather disappointing. Although the value of clinical audit being a voluntary activity was recognized, the PAC considered that the Scottish Office should set targets and timescales for involvement by all health care professionals in the process.

The Committee also considered that the Scottish Office should give guidance to purchasers and providers of health care on what should constitute regular and systematic audit. They recommended that there should be a means of systematically disseminating examples of best practice in this area.

On the costs and benefits, the PAC welcomed the intention of the Scottish Office to set up a national database of what had changed as a result of clinical audit so that the benefits of the initiative could be identified. They were concerned, however, that it was difficult, if not impossible, to get a reliable estimate of the total cost of clinical audit. Although it was possible to identify the specific additional funds allocated by the Scottish Office for clinical audit, which amounted to £20 million up to 31 March 1994, the overall cost was likely to be much greater, once the cost of the time of health professionals is included.

They recommended that the Scottish Office consider ways in which they can obtain a more reliable estimate of the overall cost of clinical audit and that they initiate a cost benefit analysis of the initiative.

On integrating clinical audit into the management structure of the NHS, the PAC wanted the Scottish Office to keep under review the amount of money being spent on clinical audit by health boards and to monitor the use that purchasers were making of clinical audit to ensure appropriate standards of patient care in contracts are met. They also wanted the Scottish Office to monitor closely to ensure that the separation of purchaser and provider does not inhibit the further development of clinical audit.

The Government's response

The Government consider the recommendations which PAC have made, and publish their response in what is known as a Treasury Minute. The response to the PAC's recommendations on clinical audit in Scotland was published in February 1995[5].

The Government felt that the extent of participation in audit at the time when the NAO looked at it was reasonable, given that audit had only been introduced in 1989, and that it takes time for audit to spread from enthusiasts to the critical mass. The Government's view was that the emphasis now is on audit activity being an integral part of day-to-day practice with the information required for audit being derived from normal recording processes.

The Scottish Office has established a new Clinical Audit Resource Centre in Scotland. One of the tasks of that Centre is to assist in disseminating information and developing a computerized database, and by November 1994 details of over 2600 audit projects were already on that database and had been disseminated.

The Scottish Office is considering how far it is possible to establish the full costs of clinical audit, but it believes that considerable benefits have been produced by the audit initiative. It accepted the recommendation from PAC that it should undertake a cost benefit analysis, but considers that this is likely to be a complex and costly process until the required information base and methodology can be developed.

The Clinical Audit Resource Centre which has been established has a remit to develop methodologies for evaluating the economic costs and benefits, both financial and qualitative, of the audit process.

On integrating clinical audit into the NHS the Government expects health boards (the equivalent of health authorities in England and Wales), will monitor expenditure against benefits. The Government's view is that the important role that purchasers have in clinical audit is to ensure that the services which they contract for are subject to appropriate quality controls, and that in itself will ensure that clinical audit remains firmly on the agenda and continues to be developed.

Conclusions

What can be concluded as a result of the NAO's report, the Public Accounts Committee's examination and the Government's response on whether clinical audit does represent value for money as a national initiative? It is clear that benefits or potential benefits are being derived from clinical audit activity and, anecdotally, the NAO were able to identify these in every hospital and GP practice they visited. It is, however, very difficult at this stage to quantify these benefits in any meaningful way. Similarly, there are no reliable estimates of the total costs of clinical audit. In particular, little information is available on the amount of time that health professionals are devoting to audit, and therefore the opportunity cost of this activity.

This raises the question of whether it is really appropriate to try to put some cash values on an activity which is designed to improve quality and is also designed to be an educational process to change the culture of how health professionals approach their work. This was a question which was raised during the Public Accounts Committee hearing.

Mr Robert Maclennan MP asked if it was difficult to judge the effectiveness of clinical audit in purely cash terms. Mr Geoff Scaife, the Chief Executive of the NHS in Scotland, replied 'It is difficult, but since we're investing specific sums in a specific programme it does behove us to ask specific questions about what benefits are flowing and whether we can quantify these. Clearly the currency we often use is money in order to be able to do that'[4]. In short, although it may well be difficult to quantify, that is no excuse for not trying.

In the light of this, is it possible to make an assessment of the value for money of clinical audit? At this stage, and at national level, there are insufficient data on which to base a judgement. There is no clear picture either of the total cost, or the benefits. It is also likely to be impractical to obtain reliable information on costs retrospectively. Yet there is a clear expectation from PAC that the Government should make reasonable efforts to assess whether their investment in clinical audit represents value for money.

In practice it is likely that the assessment of costs and benefits will need to be made locally between purchasers and providers. Providing these assessments are carried out in a reasonably consistent way, it should be possible to draw on those data for national monitoring without incurring excessive additional costs, and the Scottish Office, through the Clinical Audit Resource Centre is committed to developing methodologies for evaluating costs and benefits.

The Scottish Office is already collecting data on the benefits emerging from audit projects in three categories: projects showing costed savings, projects showing value for money but unquantified, and projects showing uncosted improvements in care.

There is a need for further research on assessment of benefits arising from clinical audit. In particular many claims are made for the intangible benefits arising from clinical audit activity, such as better teamwork, and a more questioning approach to clinical work, but there is little hard evidence available yet to support these claims.

There is a need, therefore, to continue working towards an answer to the question of whether clinical audit represents good value for money. This need not necessarily require complex costly processes but will require a rigorous questioning approach on the part of purchasers and providers, clinicians and managers, seeking to develop better data on cost and benefits. This is an approach which can challenge the scepticism of the non-participant with hard evidence of the benefits of clinical audit in improved patient care, and can temper possible excesses of the enthusiast with a clear picture of the total costs, including the opportunity costs of clinical audit.

This rigorous approach and the development of appropriate methodologies for evaluating the costs and benefits of clinical audit could help direct clinical audit activity into the most productive areas and eventually demonstrate whether or not clinical audit as it is presently organized represents value for money.

References

1   National Audit Office. *Auditing clinical care in Scotland (HC 275)*. London: HMSO, 1994

2   Department of Health. *Working for patients*. London: HMSO, 1989

3   Clinical Resource and Audit Group. *The interface between clinical audit and management*. Edinburgh: Scottish Office, 1994

4   Committee of Public Accounts. *Auditing clinical care in Scotland (HC 375)*. London: HMSO, 1994

5   Treasury Minute on the 49th to 51st Reports from the Committee of Public Accounts 1993–94 (Cm 2754) London: HMSO, 1995

The traits of success in clinical audit

KIERAN WALSHE

THE HEALTH SERVICES MANAGEMENT CENTRE, BIRMINGHAM, UK

Anyone who has been involved in clinical audit in the NHS over the last five years cannot have failed to observe that while some healthcare providers have made great progress in establishing clinical audit and producing improvements in the quality of care, others have conspicuously failed to achieve much at all. It has been obvious that large variations exist in the degree of success and effectiveness with which clinical audit programmes work, however that is measured. This paper reports on the results of a study which set out to examine and understand this phenomenon. The aim was to identify the characteristics or traits of clinical audit programmes which were associated with success (or, conversely, with failure), and in so doing to offer a practical insight which those involved in clinical audit could use to improve the effectiveness of their own endeavours.

CASPE evaluation of audit

This study formed one part of a larger evaluation[1]. In 1993, CASPE Research was commissioned by the Department of Health to undertake an evaluation of the medical, nursing and therapy and clinical audit programmes in the NHS in England. This was a sizeable undertaking, with a number of separate strands or subprojects each with its own particular objectives and methods. Table 1 sets out some brief details of the principal components of the evaluation. Together, they were intended to provide a balanced and comprehensive evaluation of what was a large and complex set of interrelated programmes. While part of their function was simply to establish what was happening, by mapping and offering a structured analysis of

EVALUATING CLINICAL AUDIT: PAST LESSONS, FUTURE DIRECTIONS, EDITED BY KIERAN WALSHE, 1995.
INTERNATIONAL CONGRESS AND SYMPOSIUM SERIES NO 212 PUBLISHED BY ROYAL SOCIETY OF MEDICINE PRESS LIMITED

Table 1 *The CASPE evaluation of audit in the HCHS in England*

Aim	Report
Review the current state of knowledge about the effectiveness of clinical audit and provide a conceptual framework for the evaluation	Evaluating audit: developing a framework. London: CASPE, 1993
Identify and review current and recent research related to the evaluation of audit and quality initiatives	Evaluating audit: a review of initiatives. London: CASPE 1993
Map the progress of medical audit nationally in all healthcare provider units in England	The development of audit: findings of a national survey of healthcare provider units in England. London: CASPE, 1994
Map the involvement in audit of commissioning authorities in England	The role of the commissioner in audit: findings of a national survey of commissioning authorities in England. London: CASPE, 1994
Map and review the audit activities of the medical Royal Colleges and examine their contribution to the development of audit at provider level	The audit activities of the medical Royal Colleges and their Faculties in England. London: CASPE, 1995
Undertake a detailed review of the functioning of audit programmes at a sample of providers, to examine impact and workings of audit in detail	Provider audit in England: a review of 29 programmes. London: CASPE, 1995
Review the management and direction of the nursing and therapy audit programme at regional level	Nursing and therapy audit: a review of the regions' role. London: CASPE Research, 1995
Map the progress of the nursing and therapy audit programme nationally at provider level throughout England	A review of audit activity in the nursing and therapy professions. London: CASPE Research, 1995

audit activities and initiatives, they were also intended to address more complex questions about the impact of audit and its effectiveness.

Review of audit at twenty-nine providers

This paper draws largely on our detailed review of the progress and impact of audit at a sample of healthcare providers, which took place mainly in the first half of 1994[2]. For this part of the evaluation, we chose 29 healthcare providers from among all those in England. The criteria we used to select these providers, listed in Table 2, were designed to ensure that the sample was reasonably representative of all healthcare providers. We were especially concerned to avoid the kind of selection biases which might have resulted in the providers in the sample tending to be all those with good, developed audit programmes.

Table 2 *Criteria used to select providers for detailed review*

1. **Location.** We selected 2 providers from each of the 14 old NHS regions, and one special health authority.
2. **Provider type.** We chose from among providers of acute, community and combined services to ensure our sample reflected the proportions of these providers in England.
3. **Provider size.** Data on provider size (in terms of annual revenue income) was used to ensure that an appropriate range of providers was included in the sample.
4. **Level of audit activity.** Data from an earlier national postal survey of healthcare providers was used to separate providers into those with apparently low, medium and high levels of audit activity and part of our sample was drawn from each group.
5. **Size of audit programme.** Again, national survey data was used to identify the size of audit programmes (through budgetary and staffing information) and the sample was drawn to include a spread of sizes.
6. **Response to postal survey.** The survey achieved a response rate of 79%, and our sample drew on both responders and non-responders to the survey in appropriate proportions.

Once the providers had been chosen, they were all contacted and asked to take part in our study. Only one provider refused, for reasons to do with local organizational turbulence rather than the audit programme itself, and we sought and found a substitute provider to take its place.

We collected a wide range of written documentation from each provider in the sample, including Trust annual reports and profiles; audit annual reports and forward plans for the current and previous years; and minutes of audit committee meetings for the last year. We then arranged to visit each provider, usually for two days, during which we undertook tape recorded, confidential interviews with around 10 key individuals. Generally, this included the chief executive, chair of the audit committee, audit coordinator, director of nursing/quality; lead clinicians for audit in selected specialties; a junior doctor; a doctor with little interest or involvement in audit locally; a finance manager; and a representative of the provider s main purchasing authority. We also held a widely advertized open meeting, to which anyone with an interest in audit could come, and we collected some quite detailed information about a selection of specific audit projects. At the end of each visit, we gave the provider some informal feedback on their audit programme as we saw it, which helped us to check what we had found with them and also gave them some benefit from what was an arduous and time-consuming external review.

Defining success in audit

This part of our evaluation had two main aims. Firstly, we wanted to find out *how successful* the audit programmes at these providers had been, and to draw some conclusions from that about the success of the audit programme in the wider NHS. Secondly, we wanted to identify *the reasons why* some audit programmes were more successful than others, so that participants in the audit process could learn from the experience of others and improve the quality and effectiveness of their own audit programmes. But to do either of these things, we first had to define what we meant by a successful audit programme. We did this by choosing four key components or benchmarks of success, which are shown in Table 3. A successful audit programme should, we believe, be directed at achieving quality improvement; be valued and respected by stakeholders in the programme; cover the full range of clinical services and professions that the provider concerned contains; and be producing documented, demonstrable improvements in the quality of care. We chose these four benchmarks of success in audit in part because we believed they were primarily concerned with the outputs or products of an audit programme, rather than its processes. We did not want to link our definition of success to any particular way of organizing audit, or the use of specific systems or techniques. In short, we wanted to measure success in terms of results (not activity), and then to see what contributed to or hindered that success.

We found a very few providers whose audit programmes were clearly very successful and could genuinely be said to be achieving most or all of the four benchmarks of success set out above. They were still capable of doing better, but they were already doing very well indeed. Most of

Table 3 *Benchmarks of success in audit*

---

1. Directed at quality improvement

    A successful audit programme should be designed to bring about improvements in the quality of care. The primary focus of the activities that make up the programme should be quality improvement, and the programme resources should be deployed with that goal in mind.

2. Valued and respected by stakeholders

    A successful audit programme should have credibility and value from the perspectives of a number of important stakeholders in the programme, including but not limited to those who participate in audit activities. There should be evidence that clinicians of different professions, managers, purchasers, and patients all value the programme for its achievements in quality improvement.

3. Covering the full range of provider services, departments and professions

    A successful audit programme should involve all the services, departments and professions in the provider it serves. There should be evidence of activity and quality improvement across a wide range of areas, not just in some or a few.

4. Producing documented, demonstrable improvement in the quality of care

    A successful audit programme should be able to demonstrate its impact on the quality of care, through documented changes in clinical and organizational practice which led to significant and lasting improvements in the quality of care delivered to patients.

---

the providers we visited had audit programmes which had made fair progress in achieving perhaps two or three of the four benchmarks, but which clearly had substantial room for improvement in many areas. A substantial minority of providers had programmes which could not be said to have achieved any of the four benchmarks of success. In essence, their audit programmes had failed or were failing, and there was a need for action if this was to change.

Whether or not the progress made by clinical audit programmes towards our four success benchmarks is cause for celebration or concern depends on one's point of view. If one expected that, after three or four years of experience, providers should have largely established effective clinical audit programmes which were demonstrably good value for money, then our findings are disappointing because very few providers had achieved anything like that level of success. On the other hand, if one's expectations of providers' audit programmes were somewhat lower, and one hoped to see some form of audit in every provider, involving most or all doctors in audit activities, raising the profile and priority of clinical audit, and improving general levels of understanding and attitudes towards audit, then our findings might seem more encouraging. Certainly we found that all those things had happened, albeit to different degrees in different providers.

Our visits to healthcare providers certainly confirmed the assertion made at the start of this paper: that large variations exist in the degree of success or effectiveness achieved by clinical audit programmes. By identifying the reasons for these variations, through our documentation reviews, interviews and observation, we hoped to find ways in which those with less successful audit programmes could improve their performance.

Traits of success in clinical audit

We identified seven key characteristics of successful audit programmes, which are listed in Table 4. We termed them *critical success factors* because it seemed from the providers we visited that their presence or absence was a critical determinant of whether or not their audit programme achieved the four benchmarks of success set out above in Table 3.

Although the Table defines the critical success factors in overview, it helps to explain their importance if we consider some real examples from the providers we visited.

Clinical leadership seemed to be the most important single determinant of an audit programme's success. While all audit programmes were led by the clinician who chaired the audit committee (virtually always a doctor), some of these individuals were distinctly less effective as leaders than others. In part, this was to do with the kind of person who led the audit programme— their position, background, standing and so on. However, it was also to do with how they saw

Table 4 *Critical success factors for clinical audit programmes*

1.	Clinical leadership	Senior clinician; multidisciplinary support; informal and formal authority; informed and educated; committed; management ability.
2.	Vision, strategy, objectives and planning	Vision of the mission; consistency and coherence; link to strategy and objectives; link to action plans; communication to the organization.
3.	Audit staff and support	High calibre of staff; right skill mix; central audit department organization; training; rewards and recognition; staff development
4.	Structures and systems	Business planning for audit department; structured approach to audit projects; records and documentation of audit activity; systems for monitoring and reporting; limited and carefully controlled IT investment
5	Training and education	Aimed at raising awareness, changing attitudes, developing skills and building teams; continuing programme of training; open and easy access; range of approaches to delivery
6	Understanding and involvement	Communication; leadership and influencing; resources and support; time; incentives and sanctions
7	Organizational environment	Relationships between managers and clinicians and between professions; links between audit and the organization; quality strategy; organizational structure; geography; relations with purchasers.

their role, how much effort they put in, and what they actually did. Successful audit programmes tended to be led by Chairs of audit committees who were senior clinicians, respected by their peers and by members of clinical professions other than their own. They had authority within the organization, both because of who they were and because of the positions they held or had held. For example, we met one Chair who over a long career at the hospital had chaired the medical staff committee, been on the management team, been a health authority member, and held almost every important medical staff position. He knew everyone, and could use his formal and informal authority to make things happen. We met another Chair who had been a consultant for about six months, and was the most junior consultant in his specialty. He had been given the job of audit Chair when he arrived, because no-one more senior wanted it. It is not difficult to imagine which of these two Chairs was more effective in taking clinical audit forward. Successful Chairs tended to be well informed about audit, to have taken the trouble to learn about audit, to be genuinely committed to the concepts and intentions of audit, and to have some managerial ability and experience.

When we asked what the goals or purposes of the clinical audit programme were, the people we interviewed at providers with successful audit programmes tended to be able to answer easily, with clearly stated aims which matched each other. In contrast, at one poorly performing provider we got six quite different answers, each tinged with uncertainty and self-doubt, from six interviewees. It was evident that at providers with successful audit programmes there was an explicit vision of what the audit programme was there to do, which had been communicated to everyone involved and which was kept to consistently. In other words, the programme seemed to be a coherent whole, rather than a disparate assortment of activities. We coined the term *vision, strategy, objectives, planning* to describe the kind of strategic direction that good audit programmes demonstrated. Not only did it involve a clear vision and a coherent strategy, there also needed to be mechanisms for translating that overall direction into short and medium term actions. This meant that forward plans, timetables and progress reviews were used to keep the programme on track.

The third critical success factor we identified was *audit staff and support*. Successful audit programmes had good audit staff, who were well qualified for the often complex and demanding tasks they faced. These providers had recognized that audit staff were an expert resource which clinicians should use for advice and support, not clerical assistants, note pullers or data entry clerks. They had organized their audit staff into a small department, thought carefully about the range of skills that service needed, given training where it was required, and treated audit staff as valued and important members of the team.

We were surprised to find that many audit programmes faltered because quite basic *structures and systems*, necessary for the effective running of any small department or organization, were missing. The audit department, like any other, needed to have some form of business plan. There had to be simple systems for managing the workload of audit projects, prioritizing and timetabling work, and dealing with routine administration. Audit projects needed to be selected carefully, planned properly, implemented effectively and then evaluated afterwards. In order to report on the development of clinical audit within the provider, the audit department needed to have mechanisms for monitoring and reporting activities in specialties and departments. Perhaps because some audit departments were managed by audit Chairs and audit coordinators with limited experience in similar roles, these basic structures and systems often did not exist.

The fifth critical success factor was *training and education*, and it was in this area more than any other that we found it hard to identify any really successful providers. This was not because the providers we visited had tried to mount training and education related to audit and had not succeeded. Rather, it seemed to be because they had often failed to recognize the need for training, let alone attempt to meet it. Where we did see training and education being offered, albeit somewhat sporadically, it seemed to us to help meet four key needs. It raised awareness of audit, and brought clinicians into contact with the ideas and methods of audit and quality improvement. It changed attitudes, helping to persuade sceptical and hostile clinicians to get involved. The most direct purpose of training was to develop skills which, despite their professional training and background, many clinicians did not possess already. Finally, training was an important way to build audit teams and structures, because when staff from different professions within a specialty or department were brought together for training it helped to establish links and created a nascent audit group.

Securing the *understanding and involvement* of clinicians within the provider was, in part, achieved by some of the critical success factors already described. However, it also seemed to be an important factor in its own right. It required good communication, training and leadership as has already been discussed. However it also needed resources, support and time to be devoted to audit by the organization, and there needed to be appropriate incentives and sanctions in place to encourage participation and to deal with non-participation.

The last critical success factor related to the organization itself, and the *organizational environment* in which the audit programme was developing. In short, we found that healthy, well managed providers, with good personal and professional relationships among staff and good relations with purchasers were able to establish better audit programmes. In contrast, dysfunctional organizations with a history of internal and external conflict and dissent found establishing audit just as difficult as they found doing most things. Of course, this meant that the organizations likely to be in most need of audit and quality improvement were probably the least able to make it happen.

These seven critical success factors were not independent of each other. We observed that they tended to cluster, in that providers who were good at one thing to do with audit were often good at another. For example, good leadership, vision, strategy and planning often went together. Good audit staff and support was often found with good structures, systems, training and education. This clustering effect tended to polarize providers into those with very good or very poor audit programmes, and it may have accounted for the wide variations in performance in audit that we observed between providers. We speculated that audit programmes tended towards either a spiral of success (in which effective audit led to quality improvements, which staff recognized and so became more enthusiastic about audit, and so on) or a spiral of decline (in which ineffective audit achieved little and wasted staff time, so destroying their initial enthusiasm, and making it progressively harder to secure clinical support and participation).

The agenda for action

It is easier to advocate change than to make it happen. Turning poor, ineffectual audit programmes into successful, effective ones is challenging, but it is the purpose of this paper to argue that it is *not* that difficult. Reviewing the list of critical success factors we identified in our study shows that most of them are amenable to change, and that the power to change often lies with those involved in the clinical audit process. Moreover the changes that are needed are not complex in themselves. In other words, if the will to change, an awareness of the need for change and an understanding of the direction of change are there, then clinical audit programmes should be able to improve—in some cases, dramatically. Those involved in poorly organized, ineffective clinical audit programmes have to take at least some of the responsibility for those failings. More constructively, they have to recognize and use their power to make those programmes more effective.

Conclusions

Since the introduction of medical audit in 1989, the level of understanding and expertise in clinical audit and quality improvement has grown tremendously. The first five years of formal, systematic and mandatory audit in the NHS have been a learning experience, and as our study shows, some providers have learnt more quickly than others. The best audit programmes among the 29 we visited seemed to confirm that clinical audit is a worthwhile and important investment, and it should be a continuing part of clinical practice and healthcare delivery in the NHS. At the worst audit programmes we saw, funding and clinicians' initial enthusiasm had both been frittered away and there was understandable disillusion with the whole process of clinical audit. In the current environment, in which funding for clinical audit is no longer ringfenced and the nature of audit is left largely for purchasers and providers to determine locally, poorly organized, ineffective clinical audit programmes cannot be expected to survive. They must either change, or face disinvestment. However, successful clinical audit programmes should continue to grow and flourish, because they can demonstrate their ability to produce significant and lasting improvements in the quality of patient care.

Acknowledgement

This research was supported by a grant from the Department of Health. It could not have taken place without the contributions and involvement of the other members of the research team, who were Madeleine Willmot, Moira Rumsey, Judy Foster, Jim Coles, Yvette Buttery, Jenny Bennett and Moyra Amess. Thanks also to all those at the providers we visited.

References

1   Walshe K, Coles J. Medical audit: evaluation needed. *Qual Health Care* 1993; 2: 189–90

2   Buttery Y, Walshe K, Rumsey M, Amess M, Bennett J, Coles J. *Provider audit in England: a review of twenty-nine programmes.* London: CASPE Research, 1995

Does clinical audit improve the quality of nursing care?

ALISON KITSON, GILL HARVEY AND CLARE MORRELL

RCN DYNAMIC QUALITY IMPROVEMENT PROGRAMME
THE NATIONAL INSTITUTE FOR NURSING, RADCLIFFE INFIRMARY, OXFORD, UK

This paper describes the work of the Royal College of Nursing (RCN) in developing standard setting and audit in nursing practice. It identifies the underpinning philosophy of the RCN approach, namely a locally-driven, clinically-focused method which accentuates the change management and action phase of the audit cycle. Three studies undertaken between 1989–95 looking at the effectiveness of the RCN's approach are described briefly. Common lessons to be learnt are drawn from these studies and points for further exploration are identified. Co-ordination of effort and clarity of purpose, emerged as the central building blocks of any audit activity. Also the need to recognize the interplay between local, organizational and strategic level was identified. Finally there were no quick fixes or short cuts to successful audit which demonstrated improvements in patient care.

Introduction

Throughout the late 1980s and early 1990s there have been many developments in the methodology and application of audit, particularly within specific disciplines, e.g. nursing, medicine and professions allied to medicine. Despite the growing interest given to health care quality and audit both in terms of time and resources, questions continue to be raised about the effectiveness of audit and its ability to change practice and improve patient care[1].

There are at least four reasons why the effectiveness of audit continues to be questioned. Perhaps the central issue is still one of how to translate concepts of quality and audit in a way

EVALUATING CLINICAL AUDIT: PAST LESSONS, FUTURE DIRECTIONS, EDITED BY KIERAN WALSHE, 1995.
INTERNATIONAL CONGRESS AND SYMPOSIUM SERIES NO 212 PUBLISHED BY ROYAL SOCIETY OF MEDICINE PRESS LIMITED

that is meaningful to those delivering the service and which ultimately makes a difference to the quality of patient care. Other reasons include the conceptual clarity with which practitioners understand the underlying values and beliefs upon which quality and audit are based, methodological issues and having to put audit into a health care system awash with change.

The history and traditions of how individual professional groups have come to understand the concepts and methods of quality and audit have a significant effect on how it is used. Harvey[2] has outlined three models of quality including an individual approach, quality through inspection and quality as involvement and collaboration. Ellis and Whittington[3] also point out that whether groups have chosen to get involved in quality or whether it has been 'forced upon them' has a big effect on how concepts and methods are adopted.

Understanding the practical elements of standard setting and audit are relatively straightforward. Descriptions of best or desired practice are written in the form of protocols, standards or criteria; these descriptions, ideally derived from research-based knowledge, and incorporating local values and adaptations are the measurement criteria against which practice is judged. Data are collected using charts, patient, nursing and medical notes, observation or interview techniques, analysis and interpretation, followed with appropriate action. This final phase has come under a lot of scrutiny[4] and has been viewed as the missing and most vital link to ensuring that audit is effective.

The importance of understanding the process of implementing change is gaining prominence[5]. Given the large scale changes within health care generally, the effectiveness of audit and improving patient care has to be seen as just one of a number of possible factors that could have made a difference. Therefore being able to say that audit does improve practice is a very difficult question to answer yet none-the-less essential to ask.

Nursing quality and audit

The Royal College of Nursing (RCN) like a number of the medical royal colleges has had a central role to play in introducing the concepts and methods of quality and audit to its members. Three distinct phases within the RCN's activity on quality and standards can be identified. It began with the Study of Nursing Care research project in the late 1960s under the leadership of Baroness Jean McFarlane[6] and was followed by the setting up of a Standards of Care Working Committee in the late 1970s. The recommendations from this working committee[7,8] led to the third and present phase of development namely the creation of a specific quality improvement programme established in 1985.

The central theme of all the RCN's work on quality has been to provide support and direction to nurses on how they can give better patient care. The present programme has undertaken a number of tasks to achieve this including the development of a philosophy and framework for quality improvement[9], developing a standard setting and audit system to improve care[10,11], developing national specialist standards and guidelines[12] and undertaking research and development[2,13-18,22].

Despite the apparent activity the question must still be asked whether the RCN's efforts have been effective in improving patient care. From the point of view of uptake of ideas we know that the Standards of Care work from 1985 was very popular and spread rapidly throughout the service. By 1988 over half of all District Health Authorities were identifying they were using the RCN Standard Setting System as one method of evaluating care[19]. This activity within nursing came before the Government White Paper[20] making medical audit mandatory across the health service. One of the consequences of this was that nursing audit activities were not formally supported when they first started and indeed it was not until 1991 that central audit monies were allocated to nursing and therapy audit activity.

The development of nursing audit, despite the efforts of the RCN, during the early 1990s was perceived as outside the mainstream activity. Regardless of the fact that the work was built on the foundation of local ownership, patient centred audit and control by practitioners the connections between nursing audit and medical audit were difficult to make. The methodological approach adopted by nurses varied only slightly from the main medical audit models put forward[21]. Such differences included the use of a mix of structure, process and outcome criteria to describe best practice; reliance on a trained facilitator to work with a local group on setting standards and auditing practice utilizing a range of data collection methods and using staff to collect and analyse audit data. Some of these differences were ideologically based—use of facilitator and small group method; some were logistical—use of staff to collect audit data due to lack of formal audit support at that time.

In order to evaluate the impact of the RCN Quality Improvement Strategy a series of research studies have been undertaken to see whether the work has had beneficial effects. From 1989 to 1995, six studies have been undertaken (see Table 1). Three will be discussed in this paper. They include the ODySSSy project which evaluated the effect of a practitioner based quality improvement system (Dynamic Standard Setting System) on nursing practice and patient outcomes[17], a study by Harvey[2] looking at how quality improvement systems are implemented and finally a review of whether and how the RCN quality and audit work has been integrated into wider organizational initiatives and clinical audit[22].

Table 1 *Summary of Royal College of Nursing Dynamic Quality Improvement Programme research activity*

Title	Project outline	Project staff	Funding
Which way to Quality? A study of the implementation of four quality assurance tools	Study undertaken between 1987–89 to evaluate the implementation of four commonly applied quality assurance instruments in nursing: Monitor, Qualpacs, locally devised nursing audits and a patient satisfaction questionnaire 'What the Patient Thinks'	Gill Harvey Alison Kitson	Royal National Pension Fund for Nurses
The Impact of a Nursing Quality Assurance Approach, the Dynamic Standard Setting System (DySSSy) on Nursing Practice and Patient Outcomes (The ODySSSy Project)	Study undertaken between 1989–92 to evaluate the effect of implementing a practitioner based quality improvement system (DySSSy) on nursing practice and patient outcomes in an acute surgical setting	Alison Kitson Gill Harvey Sophie Hyndman Fahera Sindhu Paul Yerrell	Department of Health
Nutritional Standards and the Older Adult: The development of guidelines for the nutritional care of older adults in continuing care	Study undertaken from 1992–94 to devise multi-professional national standards for the nutritional care of older adults in continuing care. Following a systematic review of the literature, a consensus conference was held and the standards were piloted in practice. This project is currently being followed up with a 12 month study to evaluate the implementation of the nutritional standards in practice.	Lesley Duff Alison Kitson	Royal College of Nursing
		Alison Loftus-Hills Lesley Duff	Department of Health
Nursing Quality: An evaluation of key factors in the implementation process	Post-graduate research study undertaken from 1988–92 to evaluate the implementation of three of the most commonly applied nursing quality systems in the UK (Monitor, Qualpacs, DySSSy) and identify key factors in the implementation process that could predict positive programme outcomes	Gill Harvey	Royal College of Nursing
Are Non-Pharmacological Nursing Interventions for the Management of Pain Effective? A meta-analysis	Post-graduate research study undertaken from 1991–94, involving a meta-analysis of non-pharmacological nursing interventions for pain management	Fahera Sindhu	Royal College of Nursing
The Reality of Practitioner Based Quality Improvement	Study undertaken during 1994 to review the implementation of practitioner led approaches to health care quality, focusing particularly on the use of the Dynamic Standard Setting System (DySSSy) in the light of NHS reforms and the subsequent emphasis on quality evaluation, clinical effectiveness and multi-professional clinical audit	Clare Morrell Gill Harvey Alison Kitson	Royal College of Nursing

A discussion of common themes emerging from these studies will elucidate whether the efforts of the RCN programme have had an impact on quality.

The ODySSSy Project

The ODySSSy Project[17] was a three-and-a-half year study started in 1989, funded by the Department of Health, to evaluate the effect of a practitioner based quality improvement system (DySSSy) on nursing practice and patient outcomes. It was set up as a controlled trial, with quasi-experimental and descriptive features. Ten acute surgical wards in five district general hospitals were selected to take part in the study. Wards were randomly allocated into experimental (those who were going to set and audit standards using the RCN system) and control (those wards who would continue as normal) conditions. The clinical intervention on which standards were to be written was post-operative pain management.

Data were collected over a period of 14 months from patients and nurses on the wards and from the standard and audit groups and facilitators. A total of 1545 patients were involved in the study, 200 nurses and a total of 68 standard setting and audit meetings were observed.

A member of the research team worked with two facilitators chosen by each hospital to train the experimental ward nursing teams to set and audit their post-operative pain management standard. A period of 14 months was considered more than enough time to enable staff to learn how to audit their care, to implement the new standards and to make any improvements following implementation and audit. A timetable indicating a three-month period for introducing and training staff, four months for researching and agreeing the standard followed by four months to implement and audit the standard was considered sufficient to achieve the task. Groups were encouraged to meet regularly for one and a half to two hours every two to four weeks, guided and supported by the local facilitators. The facilitators met every three months with a member of the research team who advised them on facilitation skills and techniques.

Results

All five of the standard setting wards succeeded in writing a standard; three succeeded in implementing and auditing it in the time period; one had audited it but had not fully implemented the improvements and one ward which had the most meetings and most group members got as far as writing the standard.

Group processes and role of facilitator

Achieving the task was found to be linked with group membership characteristics and qualities of the local facilitators. Membership of the standard setting groups was representative of the wider nursing team on the three wards which had successfully completed the task. Also the facilitators on these wards had prior experience with standard setting, quality improvement or practice development. Thus getting the job done was linked with selecting a representative ward group and ensuring that facilitators had a level of basic knowledge before commencing. Those facilitators who had no previous knowledge found the process too difficult to accomplish within the research period. Common problems identified by the facilitators included role ambiguity between group members and facilitators, tension over group leadership, lack of skills and knowledge, losing group momentum and group members generally being passive and not arguing points through.

Changes in nursing practice

There was evidence of reported changes in practice in two of the five wards. Areas where reported change had taken place in the way nursing care was being delivered included the consistent use of pain assessment charts, regular communication of pain information to team members and communication of pain management practice between wards and other departments. Patients were also found to be more vocal and assertive regarding their own pain management, there was greater consistency between day and night nursing care and greater awareness of the need for multidisciplinary collaboration on three of the five wards. These were the same wards which had completed the task and had experienced facilitators.

The effects on patients

Improvements in post-operative pain management were evident in three of the five experimental wards. In the other two experimental wards and all the control wards, no apparent changes were observed. Only one of the three wards that showed improvements over time had statistically significant results on the pain measures when univariate chi-squared association and linear trend was tested. The absence of strong statistical evidence for the effect of standard setting on quality patient care was explained by a number of the process observations. Firstly the noted improvements in patients' pain scores over the 14-month period in three of the five wards were not linear over time and on analysing the group process data strong links between peaks and troughs in patient pain levels were found with specific observations in groups. The fluctuating nature of the improvement meant that overall effects were small. That the fluctuations in patient scores corresponded to documented events in the

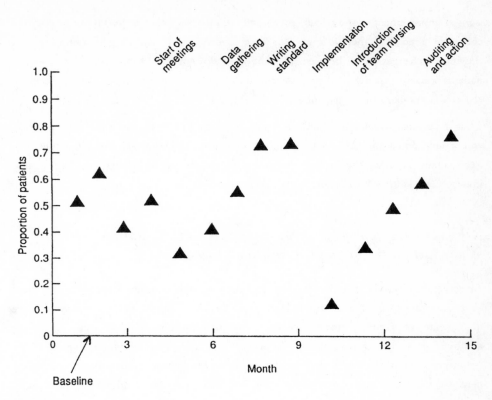

Figure 1

Changes in patient pain levels linked to group processes (as illustrated by the proportion of patients reporting their pain score at a level of 0–3 on a 10-point graphic rating scale)

groups, and in one case to the introduction of a new style of nursing to the ward, indicated that quality improvement is mediated as much through staff morale and motivation as it is by presentation of factual data. Figure 1 provides one example of how changes in patient pain levels were linked to group processes.

Overall however it was concluded that the RCN system can be used to improve patient care but that its effect is not strong: there are many variables that will dilute the effect. These include group composition and motivation, preparation and training of facilitators, anticipating optimum time for achieving the task and providing staff with feedback on how their behaviour and actions influence patients' experience of care.

The three wards which showed improvements in practice and patient outcomes were all located in hospitals with explicit commitment to quality improvement as an organizational goal. The two remaining experimental wards showing no improvement were in hospitals without explicit commitment to quality improvement. That none of the control wards showed signs of improvement over the study period indicates that, despite a supportive organizational culture in three areas, there is a need for direct involvement of staff in quality improvement activities if changes are to be seen. In addition to documented changes in practice and in patients' general experience of pain, staff in the three wards where improvements occurred reported a number of personal and professional developments.

Thus in considering whether audit works the ODySSSy Project indicates that both the local and organizational contexts have to be considered before reaching conclusions. The following two studies look at the wider organizational aspects of integrating nursing quality improvement systems into mainstream quality initiatives.

Achieving improvement through quality: an evaluation of key factors in the implementation process

The second study to be described involved an evaluation of how quality improvement systems have been implemented in nursing[2]. Harvey's study specifically focused on how systems are implemented in practice and with what effect, from the perspective of nursing staff experiences and their perception of the systems' effectiveness as a means of improving patient care. If a number of key factors could be detected during the implementation process that were found or perceived to have an effect on the programme outcomes then these could serve as benchmarks for future quality initiatives.

At the time of undertaking the study (1988–1992) three of the most commonly applied nursing quality systems in the UK were Monitor[23], the Quality Patient Scare Scale (Qualpacs)[24] and the RCN Dynamic Standard Setting System[11]. These were identified through two successive surveys undertaken in 1987 and 1988[19,25].

A three-stage evaluation design was used, incorporating a range of descriptive and exploratory methods. A series of 14 case studies on the implementation of each of the three systems in a number of different sites (five Monitor, four Qualpacs and five DySSSy) were used to obtain general descriptive data on how staff found the systems to work with. Then a comparative evaluation of the systems was undertaken evaluating the context within which the systems were introduced, the experiences of staff and the outcomes achieved by the implementation. This led to the identification of common themes and key success factors within the implementation process. The third stage involved a comparison of the findings from stage two with experiences of other facilitators involved in implementing quality systems.

A range of qualitative methods were used to collect data including interviews and observation of staff during the implementation process. Data were collected from ward sisters, staff nurses, nurse managers, quality co-ordinators and facilitators working in 14 different hospitals throughout England. Data were analysed using a process of content analysis to produce descriptive accounts of the implementation process within each of the 14 sites.

Results

Analysis of the data revealed a number of sequentially important factors within the implementation process. These include system-related, context related, practical and philosophical issues of implementation.

System-related factors

Implementation was found to be influenced by the way the system had been constructed. At one end of the continuum was a system like Monitor which characterizes a top-down or centrally controlled system. The key features of this were assessment of quality by external assessors, prior preparation of staff and explicit follow up action identified for staff by assessors. This approach is often described as a quality by inspection model[2]. At the other end of the continuum was a system like DySSSy which advocated a locally driven approach to quality, implemented by facilitators who helped staff identify standards, audit practice and take action following audit results. Teams could choose their assessor, there was very little prior preparation before assessment and action often happened before data were formally presented. In between these two extremes was Qualpacs which could be interpreted either as a centrally controlled quality system or one which enabled practitioners to be flexible and use it to their own ends.

There was evidence from the case studies of both success and failure in each system and a range of both positive and negative experiences in using them. This leads to the main conclusion of Harvey's work that it is not necessarily the system which creates success or failure but the way that it is implemented and used. Matching a range of context and practical factors with system characteristics was found to help in predicting what would work in what circumstances.

Context and practical issues

The context related to why and how the quality system was implemented. External reasons for using a quality system were less likely to achieve success than when reasons were justified by internal arguments regardless of the system chosen. Also there were situations where DySSSy was introduced in a formal, top-down way despite the fact that this was contradictory to its way of working. Similarly, Monitor and Qualpacs sometimes were found to have been introduced in a more involved and informal way, often enhancing their use.

The role and function of the implementers or facilitators was found to be central; regardless of the system such people had to be approachable and credible rather than distant or lacking clinical credibility. Success for all systems was linked to the level of penetration at local level in the organization. The expectation was that this was more easily achieved with a bottom up system such as DySSSy but it was not guaranteed. The level of feedback and action also influenced the success of the systems, open constructive and detailed dialogue invariably being more effective than instructions delivered at a distance.

The range of practical issues emerging from the analysis related to relieving staff fear and anxiety by providing adequate information, and by involving them in aspects of introducing and using the systems. The choice of change agent or facilitator to introduce the system was crucial as was their ability to offer constructive and targeted feedback. Again these factors were common to all three systems indicating core features to any implementation process.

Philosophical issues

Underpinning the system-related, contextual and practical issues of implementation, two key factors can be identified which ultimately determine the philosophy and subsequent impact of the quality programme. These are defined as ownership for quality and action to improve.

Ownership was about encouraging meaningful participation in the quality programme and giving staff a sense of control over the direction. It represented workers' understanding of the value base of the quality system and whether it valued, trusted and respected them. How these values were operationalized was seen in the level of involvement staff had with implementing and using the system. Predictably, ownership was more readily promoted by bottom up approaches to implementation notably the practitioner based methods. Pre-formulated systems such as Monitor and Qualpacs do display some limitations in that they rarely devolve ownership beyond ward sister level. However, ownership was not an automatic product of local standard and audit groups: this did depend on how the facilitator and group members identified, promoted and controlled it.

The other theme to emerge was the issue of achieving action to improve. There was no direct link between a group having ownership and their ability to take action to improve quality. Strongest predeterminants of action were feedback of the data and support at a practical and organizational level.

The analysis of the case studies found that some of the quality systems tended to promote ownership whilst others were able to generate action without a strong sense of ownership. Thus, the findings were identifying a positive outcome i.e. action when user experiences identified a lack of ownership of the process of implementation. This raises the question of whether it is necessary to try and ensure these two factors come together. Examples where the balance between ownership and action were not right reflected a number of common features: local quality systems which promoted ownership but achieved little action were often identified within organizations which espoused a collaborative approach to quality but were centrally controlling and hierarchical. Groups were given the illusion of being in control but they were unable to make practical decisions about their case that they could action.

The corollary to this quite frequently observed phenomenon was when staff were involved in an audit with little prior preparation and were given a set of results to action. Where there was top level support for this initiative resources and time were usually made available for action to take place. However, such work was generally treated with suspicion and the activity was rarely sustained.

This study looking at what makes quality systems work identified a range of practical and philosophical factors leading to more or less successful outcomes. The observations tend to support the view that systems promoting collaboration and involvement of all staff in quality achieve the best results. The logistics of achieving this, particularly with professional groups such as nursing where decision making and control have been vested in traditional hierarchies is indeed a challenge. To ensure that staff are involved, informed, supported, enabled and offered the practical help they need to change practice seems too self-evident a conclusion to reach. Yet the challenge to quality improvement seems exactly this; how do we ensure these very practical and fundamental features are built into work systems?

Quality needs to be viewed as a dynamic and organic concept, located within a general context of organizational development and change[26]. This has clear implications, both in relation to continued development of collaborative approaches to clinical audit[27,28] but also in terms of the integration of clinical audit into the quality management structure of the organization as a whole.

Similar themes have emerged from the above study to the broader conclusions from the ODySSSy project. Local success in achieving improvements in care does seem to be dependent upon wider organizational values, approaches and methods to quality, and the devolution of decision making powers to the clinical level. The challenge would seem to be how we promote the development of autonomous local units committed to the explicit strategies of the central organization.

The reality of practitioner-based quality improvement

The final study to be outlined in this trilogy is one looking at how a practitioner-based, locally-managed quality system like DySSSy has been implemented within the health care system. Particularly we were interested to find out whether the rhetoric of the need for ownership of systems (which DySSSy advocates) is quickly overtaken by the reality of traditional hierarchies and central directives for quality which in the short term tend to achieve more action. In addition to this theme we wanted to find out to what extent DySSSy did integrate with other initiatives following the health care reforms and whether it was being used for multi-professional quality improvement.

The study was undertaken during 1994. A series of semi-structured interviews with nurses who had used the RCN Dynamic Standard Setting System were conducted across the UK. A total of 28 representative sites from a cross section of members of the RCN Dynamic Quality Improvement Network were selected for investigation. The sites were chosen to include the very best, and most unexceptional ways in which nurses were utilizing the RCN's work.

The interviews with staff (key facilitators) in each site were tape recorded and field notes on the clinical areas were kept by the main researcher (CM). Data were analysed using a process of content analysis to produce descriptive accounts of how DySSSy was being implemented at a clinical and organization level and how it is moving towards clinical audit.

Results

Four main themes emerged from the data outlining what nurses found good about the system and what caused problems, what factors helped in implementing it at local level, how it was being integrated with other quality initiatives and progress toward multiprofessional clinical audit.

Mechanics of the system

Those areas where the system was working well found it had acted as a catalyst for change, it had been integrated into daily work processes, refined and adapted to local needs. Some areas had also used the local group set-up to involve patients in the writing and auditing of standards.

Most areas identified lack of time as a major drawback. The separation of the task of writing and auditing standards from the underlying philosophy of the system was also seen as problematic. Lack of clear understanding about audit, little involvement of patients and managers taking control of the process were also common problems identified in some areas.

Implementation at a clinical level

The facilitators and quality co-ordinators charged with the job of getting nursing audit into practice identified a range of factors that either helped or hindered the process. Personal characteristics of the facilitators, organizational support and executive commitment were important to local success. The personal freedom and autonomy of the facilitator and their ability to empower and motivate others and to challenge the *status quo* in a constructive way were essential factors.

Conversely, other facilitators talked about being overwhelmed, having no support, being conscripted into the post which itself had neither been clearly thought through nor properly supported. Needless to say, in such situations the effectiveness of local standard setting and audit activity was severely limited.

Integration of RCN system into other initiatives

For those units who had successfully implemented the local practitioner-based approach, the range of health reforms were seen as a challenge rather than a threat. The purchaser provider split and application for trust status had often ensured that small scale local quality initiatives started by nurses were brought to the attention of top executives. This also happened when quality strategies were required: in units where nursing standards had developed successfully, the expertise of the practitioners and facilitators were used to spread the ideas across the organization. Local staff described situations where quality specifications and health gain targets were actually including local nursing data. However, despite some examples of good practice, a fragmented approach to these various issues persisted in a majority of sites visited. Such experiences are typified by the following quote:

> 'there almost seems to be like an arm chopped off, that nursing comes on doing all its nursing things, initiating things and carrying on ... and the trust-wide developments, they go on with the Quality Assurance Manager, but as far as I know there is no strategy ... (but) I have heard it's coming ...'

An integrated approach to quality appeared to require not only clear leadership, but also the full commitment of the management team in seeing the strategy implemented and establishing a synchronous set of system and structures to support the many initiatives.

Moving to clinical audit

Those areas where nursing and medical audit were coming together in an exciting and constructive way tended to demonstrate the following characteristics: confident nurses who could state clearly the nature of their practice; involvement in joint education and training initiatives on quality and a clear strategy on how clinical audit is integrated into the mainstream business of the trust.

More typically, respondents talked about misunderstandings and tribal boundaries, products of local attitudes between professions and the histories of the introduction of audit to the different groups. Nurses' lack of confidence was identified as one factor stopping them from contributing to the clinical team. Poor communication, lack of any clear strategy and poor co-ordination were also cited frequently as major detractors from effective clinical audit. As one respondent said:

> 'Everything is what I call disparate ... the people from nursing who go to the clinical audit meetings are not the people involved in nursing audit, which is bizarre. And then again they are also not at those nursing quality meetings, so they don't really know what's going on, so everything's in limbo the whole time'

This final study again reinforces central messages of corporate strategy for quality, clear target setting and support for staff. The disparate and variable timing of the introduction of new ideas can never be controlled but it seems they should be co-ordinated and 'exploited' much more effectively. Those champions of local quality initiatives who broke through the 'glass ceiling' went on to make very valuable contributions to the corporate quality strategy. Conversely, those individuals who felt unsupported at local level were unsupported at both corporate and multi-professional level. It hardly matters whether they were using a nursing quality system or any other: the results would probably have been the same because of the underlying culture and power base of the organization.

Discussion

The studies outlined indicate that using clinical audit as a method for improving practice is neither an easy option nor a quick fix solution. It is not something that can be dispensed with a half day study session and a manual. Rather, for clinical audit to be effective one must be looking for significant changes in behaviour, attitude, roles, traditions and individual expectations. Such changes within individual practitioners must be supported by organizational changes that reflect the underlying values of participation, involvement and a commitment to continuous improvement.

From the first study it was evident that although tangible improvements in post-operative pain management were identified in three of the five control wards, the achievement and sustaining of that change was dependent upon factors other than individual knowledge and will. Similarly in Harvey's study of how nursing quality systems were implemented it was the matching of the contextual and practical factors of the organization with system characteristics that determined the success or otherwise of the implementation. This balance between local ownership and control of audit initiatives and corporate responsibility for providing direction and support at an organizational level was also brought out in the third study.

The tension between local (clinical) and organizational (corporate and strategic) issues in determining the success or otherwise of audit initiatives may be particularly pertinent to nursing. It could be that because of its traditions and management practices the nursing profession has had to struggle to ensure that its practitioners at ward level had the power and authority to initiate changes thereby improving practice. However, the quality improvement literature and particularly Berwick[29] identifies similar problems for medical and other professional groups. Thus, it would seem that one of the challenges facing all the professions is how they integrate local audit initiatives into a supportive organizational framework that gives strategic direction without compromizing the creativity, diversity and autonomy needed at local level to make things happen.

A number of positive and negative features can be identified from the studies that lead to success or failure with audit at local level. Of primary importance is that the clinical team needs support to undertake effective audit; if facilitators are used then their level of training in audit and group process skills can affect the clinical outcomes. Also the composition of the audit team was found to influence results: larger, non-representative audit teams had less success than smaller teams whose members represented the skill mix of the ward. This observation has obvious relevance to clinical audit teams.

Team motivation and morale were found to affect the way staff chose to implement the new practices. Change in practice was also found to take place immediately staff felt it was appropriate but if it had not been negotiated with others and formalized within the local pattern of events then things quickly returned to old ways. In wards where practice had been observed to change over time a number of patterns were found: the change had become the new norm; everyone knew about it; patients were also more informed and there was more discussion and collaboration with colleagues.

At local level audit was not effective when it was imposed, where tribal boundaries persisted, where there was role conflict between members of the same professional group (e.g. between trained and auxiliary nursing staff in one standard setting ward) and where staff lack confidence in their own ability to change practice. Often nursing staff complained about the lack of management support to achieve local change and a token commitment to promoting involvement and ownership at local level.

From all three studies there were consistent reports that success at local level was closely linked with support at organizational level. How concepts and practices of quality improvement and audit were introduced into organizations seemed to determine their successful uptake. In some cases systems with a strong centralist and controlling approach worked very well but only in places that needed clear boundaries and explicit instructions. In other areas the need to involve staff in meaningful participation and giving them a sense of control over events was of paramount importance.

How such sentiments are turned into operational policy is still a matter of conjecture and speculation. The need for co-ordination and planning of a whole range of health care initiatives has never been greater but there still seems to be a prevailing attitude which sees policy change as a set of tasks to be achieved without a clear understanding of how things must be synthesized.

Lessons to be learnt

From the three studies described in the paper a number of common themes have emerged: central to the effective uptake and execution of clinical audit is the need to understand how it works at different levels of the organization. At strategic level where corporate strategies for improvement exist and where the culture supports dynamic change, integration and decentralized decision making, then teams at local level have a much clearer perception of their role.

At organizational level (clinical directorate level) suitable infrastructures must be set in place which provide training to staff and help them to plan their audit activity. They must enable effective communication between departments and provide mechanisms for evaluating local activities against organizational and national targets. The clinical director's role is to support local activity by helping to incorporate audit into routines, minimize paperwork and provide local facilitation.

Table 2 *Evaluating audit*

Level within organizational structure	Strategic	Organizational (Directorate)	Clinical team
KEY FACTORS	• Corporate strategy for improvement • Strong leadership • Organizational culture supportive of change • Decentralized decision-making • Integration of managerial and professional quality	• Effective communication systems • Provision of training and support • Incorporation of audit into everyday practice • Integration of strategic and local (clinical) audit agenda	• Support to undertake audit e.g. facilitator • Facilitator with skills in audit and managing group processes • Representative audit team • Inter-professional teamwork and respect • Relevance of audit topic/ proposed changes • Management support to achieve local change

The supportive framework at strategic and organizational level (see Table 2) will ensure that local activity can be optimized. Making clinical teams effective will require training, support, a culture of devolved decision making and fast flexible communication methods. Such local change as has been demonstrated does not happen in a vacuum. The real challenge is to understand those forces which will restrain and enhance such activity. Leadership at each level is essential, together with a clear understanding of the tasks to be achieved.

Finally, the organizational activity can be supported by national bodies such as the Royal Colleges and more recently the National Centre for Clinical Audit. Jointly led by the Royal College of Nursing and the British Medical Association, this centre seeks to make clinical audit more effective by collating and disseminating audit information, providing a database of projects, offering an enquiry service and library function. The centre will also be offering support in areas such as team building, quality improvement and networking.

The flow of information and expertise from national to local level and *vice versa* is central to any long lasting, effective change. Much has been achieved through audit yet much remains to be tackled. How initiatives such as audit, clinical effectiveness, evidence based health care and so on are integrated surely are some of the most interesting challenges facing health care delivery at the moment.

References

1 Walshe K, Coles J. *Evaluating audit: developing a framework*. London: CASPE Research, 1993

2 Harvey G. *Nursing quality: An evaluation of key factors in the implementation process*. Unpublished Ph.D thesis. London: South Bank University, 1993

3 Ellis R, Whittington D. *Quality assurance in health care: a handbook*. London: Edward Arnold, 1993

4 Coles C. Making audit truly educational. *Postgrad Med J* 1990; **66**: S32–36

5 Stocking. Promoting change in clinical care. *Qual Health Care* 1992; **1**: 56–60

6 McFarlane J. *The proper study of the nurse*. London: Royal College of Nursing, 1970

7 Royal College of Nursing. *Standards of nursing care*. London: Royal College of Nursing, 1980

8 Royal College of Nursing. *Towards standards*. London: Royal College of Nursing, 1981

9 Kitson A L. *A framework for quality: a patient-centred approach to quality assurance in health care*. Harrow: Scutari, 1989

10 Kendall H, Kitson A L. Rest assured. *Nurs Times* 1986; **82**: 29–31

11 Royal College of Nursing. *Quality patient care: the Dynamic Standard Setting System*. Harrow: Scutari, 1990

12 Royal College of Nursing. *Standards of care: cancer nursing*. London: Royal College of Nursing, 1991

13 Kitson A L, Harvey G. *Bibliography of nursing: quality assurance and standards of care 1932–1987*. London: Scutari Press, 1991

14 Kitson A L, Hyndman S J, Harvey G, Yerrell P H. Problems of priority. *Nurs Times* 1990; **86**: 45–50

15 Harvey G. *Which way to quality? A study of the implementation of four quality assurance tools*. Report No. 5. Oxford: National Institute for Nursing, 1993

16 Duff L, Kitson A L, Watson R, *et al. Nutrition standards and the older adult: a report on the development of guidelines of the nutritional care of older adults in continuing care*. Oxford: Royal College of Nursing, DQI Programme, 1993

17 Kitson A L, Harvey G, Hyndman S, Sindhu F, Yerrell P. *The impact of a nursing quality assurance approach, the Dynamic Standard Setting System (DySSSy) on nursing practice and patient outcomes (the ODySSSy project)*. Report No. 4, Vols 1, 2, 3. Oxford: National Institute for Nursing, 1994

18 Sindhu F. *Are non-pharmacological nursing interventions for the management of pain effective? A meta-analysis*. Unpublished D.Phil Thesis. Oxford: University of Oxford, 1994

19 Kitson A L, Harvey G. *Nursing quality assurance directory* (2nd edition). London: Royal College of Nursing, 1988

20 Department of Health Standing Medical Advisory Committee. *The quality of medical care*. London: HMSO, 1990

21 Shaw C. Criterion based audit. *BMJ* 1990; **300**: 991–993.

22 Morrell C, Harvey G, Kitson A L. *The reality of practitioner-based quality improvement*. Report No. 11. Oxford: National Institute for Nursing, 1995

23 Goldstone L A, Ball J A, Collier M M. *Monitor: An index of the quality of nursing care for acute medical and surgical wards*. Newcastle-Upon-Tyne: Newcastle-Upon-Tyne Polytechnic Products Ltd, 1983

24 Wandelt M A, Ager J W. *Quality patient care scale*. New York: Appleton-Century-Crofts, 1974

25 Kitson A L, Harvey G. *Nursing Quality Assurance Directory*. London: Royal College of Nursing, 1987

26 Giovannetti P B, Ratner P A, Collier M M. Survey of nursing quality assurance programs in selected hospitals in Alberta, Canada. *Int J Nurs Studies* 1992; **29**: 301–13

27 Department of Health. Clinical audit: meeting and improving standards in healthcare. London: Department of Health, 1993.

28 Department of Health. *The evolution of clinical audit*. London: Department of Health, 1993

29 Berwick D. Continuous improvement as an ideal in health care. *N Engl J Med* 1989; **320**: 53–6

Clinical audit in four therapy professions: results of an evaluation

TIM PACKWOOD

DEPARTMENT OF GOVERNMENT, BRUNEL UNIVERSITY, UXBRIDGE, UK

Genesis of the research study

Outside the professional meetings and journals, discussion of audit usually leaves the impression that it is a medical preserve. This was notably the case with the White Paper, *Working for Patients* which, in the course of totally recasting the governance and organization of the NHS, made for the first time, audit a compulsory element of professional work[1].

The reality, of course, is very different. Research for the study discussed in this paper indicated how the various colleges and societies for the therapy professions had replicated the work of their medical counterparts in developing standards of care and getting audit on to the professional agenda during the 1980s[2]. Likewise, during the early 1990s professional therapists became actively engaged in audit activities in the work place. This increasing engagement in audit by all health service professions represents a successful response to policy advocated by the Department of Health. The Department has consistently sought to promote clinical audit. This, in its first manifestation, essentially meant non-medical audit. Since 1991 funds were made available for nursing and therapy audits, although the amounts available—£17.7 million over the period 1991–94, compared with £203 million for medical audit—and the allocation process—competitive bidding to regional health authorities, compared with disbursement by regions according to the number of staff employed for medical audit monies—carried a message regarding priorities[3]. Nonetheless, by 1994 the Department could report 456 nursing and therapy audits funded through its programme[4]. But Departmental

EVALUATING CLINICAL AUDIT: PAST LESSONS, FUTURE DIRECTIONS, EDITED BY KIERAN WALSHE, 1995.
INTERNATIONAL CONGRESS AND SYMPOSIUM SERIES NO 212 PUBLISHED BY ROYAL SOCIETY OF MEDICINE PRESS LIMITED

policy was always moving towards developing audit as a generic activity, capable of involving different disciplines as a common endeavour. In 1992 the Clinical Outcomes Group had been set up to advise the Chief Medical and Chief Nursing officers at the Department on 'how to give strategic direction to the development of multi-professional audit'[3].

It was entirely consistent with this approach that in 1990 the Department commissioned Professor Charles Normand and colleagues to:

- record progress in the development of clinical audit in four therapy professions (clinical psychology, occupational therapy, physiotherapy, and speech and language therapy);

- survey the published literature on clinical audit with special reference to the four professions;

- assess the degree to which there are common features of these developments;

- consider the feasibility of developing a common audit framework applicable to the four professions and, if feasible, provide a draft framework;

- identify constraints to the development of audit;

- recommend the way forward for developing audit in these professions.

The resulting Normand Report was published in 1991 and recommended that a common audit framework should be developed and tested, that the possibility of applying it more widely to other professions should be explored and that more support should be provided for audit activities[5].

The study reported below took the Normand Report as its starting point. The commission from the Department of Health was to:

- document and analyse examples of audit practice in the four therapy professions surveyed by Normand;

- produce guidelines on models of good practice upon which the four professions might base their audit activities in the future. In particular to identify whether a common core of components existed that might form the basis of a framework for multi-professional audit.

These introductory paragraphs have explained the genesis of the research. The paper continues by:

- describing the nature of the research;

- drawing attention to the changing context as regards the wider NHS;

- indicating some of the major findings;

- discussing the reasons for these results;

- suggesting how strong audit models might be developed; and, finally,

- commenting on the potential for multi-professional audit.

The research study

It can be seen from the terms of reference given above, that the research study had two components; discovery of existing audit practice and the development of future practice. The first was a task for empirical enquiry whereas the second required conceptualization and testing. These two, normally disparate sequential activities, had to be included in a single research design.

The first phase of the research comprised determining this design and beginning to undertake the literature review; a task that continued throughout the study. In the second phase a series of interviews was held with 'key informants', who could provide an account of the development of audit in the four therapy professions and suggest where in the country the latter were actively engaged in audit work. The main 'discovery' aspect of the research was to be undertaken by a series of mini-case studies of clinical audit in action, undertaken in six sites. In addition to demonstrating the existence of audit, the six sites were selected to provide examples of diversity in:

- geographical location, to allow for the impact of different regional policies;

- involvement by the four professions, each being involved in, at the minimum, one site, and being involved in both uni- and multi-professional audit activities;

- setting, to provide experience of hospital and community services;

- organization, to provide experience of trusts and directly managed units and of specialty based and functionally-based patterns of organization;

- client group, to provide examples of the effects of working with different age groups and conditions.

The third phase of the research comprised fieldwork in the six selected sites. The main methods involved were the study of relevant documentation, combined with the interview of a number of the professionals engaged in audit work together with the occupants of key positions who might be expected to play a role in using or developing audit. This latter group included general managers in provider units, purchasers and regional staff with responsibility for clinical audit. One hundred and twenty-two interviews were conducted in total, using structured interview schedules.

The fourth phase of the research comprised the analysis of the findings to enable the move into the development component. Models of audit were developed and tested; first with professional therapy staff in a further three sites and later, and after further refinement, with the Project Advisory Group. This latter, a source of advice and guidance throughout the project, consisted of senior practitioners from the professions concerned, members of research and relevant customer divisions from the Department of Health and academic advisers.

The final, and in a sense, on-going phase of the research was that of dissemination.

The research team itself was both multi-disciplinary and multi-site based. It consisted of staff working for the Centre for Evaluation of Public Policy and Practice at Brunel University and for the Nursing Research Unit at Kings College, London. The common theme was that all members had considerable experience of, and interest in, evaluative studies of the functioning of the NHS.

The context of the study

The research was undertaken over two years, 1992–1994. This timing proved important. First, although it might not have felt particularly calm to those working in it, the NHS was beginning to settle down and operate the internal market and the other provisions set out in the White Paper. This meant that it gradually became possible for the main interests in the NHS—the DoH, professional organizations, purchasers, general managers—to draw breath and think, among other things, how they wanted to use audit. Time and again interviewees made the point that audit had not been among the most controversial or contested of the changes, and it had tended to get overlooked as a result.

The growing experience of working the new NHS also meant that the implications for audit from some of the new arrangements and processes were becoming ever clearer. Audit, for example, was seen to have an increasing part in quality assurance strategies, in the contracting process and in the management of clinical directorates. Indeed as the research proceeded, attention was given to issues such as measuring outcomes and the role of purchasers in audit that had not been particularly prominent in 1991 when Normand had reported.

The second important contextual point has already been introduced. From 1992 to 1994 the Department of Health was accelerating its promotion of clinical audit as both as multi-professional activity and as an activity shaped by the internal market. The final stages of the research project coincided with an end to separate funding arrangements for medical and other forms of audit[6], coupled with the decision to allocate audit monies to purchasers on the same basis as other revenue allocations; namely according to the resident population to be served. This meant that the relevance of any models of audit that the research produced was potentially wider than the four therapy professions studied, and might be applied to all professional audit activities. However by 1994 the Department's commitment to multi-professional audit had become tempered and recognized that there was 'still a role for uni-professional audit, where professions can clearly identify their own singular contribution'[7].

This also acted to widen the potential of the research, making it relevant to include uni-professional audit within the developmental modelling.

Major findings

Evidence from the sites confirmed what informed commentators had been claiming regarding the development of audit outside medicine.

1. The scale of audit activities was impressive: 135 audit activities involving one or more of the four professions were noted in the six main fieldwork sites, with a further 49 in the three sites used for testing the models.

2. Applying Donabedian's structure, process, outcomes framework for categorizing the review of health care[8] most audits focused on the process of care, rather than on structure or on outcomes.

3. If a distinction is made between bounded audits, focusing directly on patient care, and more diffuse audits, concerned with how that care is managed and organized, audits undertaken by the four professions were fairly evenly divided between the two categories.

4. Twice as many audits were uni-professional in their membership than were multi-professional. But there were no significant differences between the two in terms of either Donabedian's' framework (2 above) or engagement in bounded or diffuse audits (3 above).

5. The majority of audits were criteria-based, applying specific criteria that could be compared, either prospectively or retrospectively, to actual practice. In many cases the audits were, themselves, being used to test or determine appropriate criteria.

6. While attempts were frequently made to audit the outcomes of care in respect of individual patients, it was proving much harder to do so for services as a whole. And the difficulties were exacerbated if the audit was multi-professional. Whereas it was feasible

for members of different disciplines to agree and establish common goals in respect of the care of individual patients, the common frameworks of process and knowledge required to jointly agree desired service outcomes did not exist.

7.   It was the professional service managers, the lead or chief therapists or the director of the discipline, who provided the drive and leadership for the majority of audit activities. But, not surprisingly, this was more the case for uni-professional than for multi-professional audits. The latter tended to be initiated from 'the bottom-up', by practitioner teams, or from 'the top down', by general managers. The professional service managers could be classified as 'middle management' within the provider units and they used audit as an aid to the management process. The audits they initiated were more likely to be concerned with process than with either structure or outcomes, and with diffuse rather than with bounded audits.

The missing links

In a sense, the description of audit undertaken by the four professions sketched out above conforms to a familiar evolutionary pattern. Audit commences on 'the safer ground', with what is known best—the processes of care applied to individual patients—before moving to less familiar and more contestable areas—concerned with structure and outcomes of care. Similarly it commences within one discipline, whose members share similar frameworks of knowledge and work processes, before risking the involvement of other disciplines with different frameworks.

The research shows that uni-disciplinary audit by the therapy professions has developed strong roots. The difficulties in extending and combining their activities can be thought of in two ways.

The first of these employs the familiar image of the audit cycle, or spiral[9,10] with its progressive stages of activity (Figure 1). Consideration of the application of this cycle in practice provokes two observations.

First, progression around the cycle involves both time and planning. Earlier study of the implementation of medical audit suggested that audit meetings used to be regarded as discrete activities and there were problems in progressing issues around the various stages[11]. And clearly, if issues are fully audited there are limits to the number that can be accommodated at any one time.

Second, completion of the various stages in the cycle is likely to involve interaction with other cycles of activity. In their work, therapy professionals frequently follow a patient care cycle;

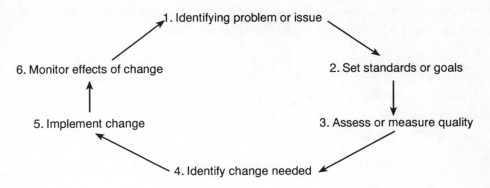

Figure 1
The clinical audit cycle

moving between assessment of condition, planning treatment, implementing planned treatment and evaluation. Experience of the individual patient care cycle can feed into stage one (identification of problems or issues) in the audit cycle. Stage two of the audit cycle (set standards or goals) may also involve a cycle of activity of debate, drafting and testing of standards while stage five (implementing change) may likewise require a cycle of debate, planning and implementation. The existence of these associated cycles of activity, as depicted in Figure 2, complicates the audit process. The staff involved are not necessarily the same, as, for example when change has to be sanctioned by managers outside the profession concerned

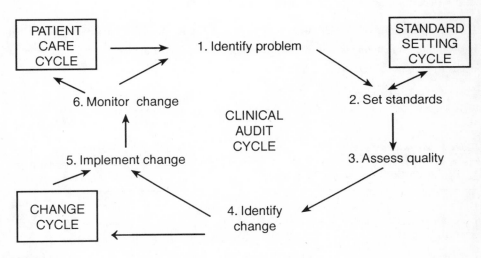

Figure 2
Clinical audit and associated cycles

or when other disciplines are closely involved in the patient care cycle, and the communication and negotiation required all adds to the time taken by the audit.

The second way of thinking of the difficulties in extending audit activities makes the same point in a different way. It has to be recognized that there are now a number of different stakeholders in the NHS with an interest in audit, beyond the professionals directly engaged in caring for and treating patients. And, further, these interests are substantially different as between different groups. The main groupings consist of:

- professional staff, concerned with the quality of care provided to individual patients;

- professional service managers, concerned with the quality of their service;

- general managers in provider units, concerned with the quality of total service provided by the institution;

- purchasers, concerned with the quality of service received by the population served.

Different perspectives of quality were usefully categorized in a recent evaluation of Total Quality Management in the NHS[12]. This study distinguished between:

- the technical mode, concerned with the specialist quality of processes of care;

- the generic mode, concerned with common aspects of quality in the way that work is organized and managed, as applied by whole services, a department or management unit;

- the systemic mode, concerned with the quality of a comprehensive and integrated set of services to meet the health needs of a local population.

If this categorization of concerns with quality is matched with the different staff groupings that have an interest in audit, as in Table 1, it can be seen that from a managerial perspective audit needs to be multi-functional.

Table 1 *Perspectives of audit*

Staff group	Concern	Mode of quality assurance
Professional staff	Services to individual patients	Technical
Professional service managers	Service to patients	Technical Generic
General managers	Services provided by sub-unit or unit	Generic Systemic
Purchasers	Services available, individually and collectively, to the local population	Technical, Generic, Systemic

In other words, it has to play in a larger arena than that represented by the professional practitioners alone and it has to be concerned with more than technical process.

Making the links

Analysing the structural and processual factors that currently shape clinical audit is helpful in considering how it might be assisted to develop and extend its function.

First, there appears to be a key role for the professional service managers. Unlike the case with medical audit, which operates under the constraints and opportunities afforded by clinical freedom[13], audit in the therapy professions has been imposed hierarchically. This has advantages in terms of clear leadership. Also, accountability for audit follows the same path as accountability for work; as opposed to setting-up separate hierarchies of accountability for quality, as has been found to be the case with some of the TQM initiatives[12]. The disadvantage is that engagement in the audit process calls for a democratic mode of working, for peer reviews, with staff participating on the basis of their knowledge and experience without feeling threatened by what is revealed. This fits less happily with managerial accountability, since the latter always remains, however democratic the style of working adopted by the manager. And this sense of audit as a threat is exacerbated to the extent that service managers explicitly use audit results as a means of staff appraisal, as was the case with some of the projects studied.

The potential importance of the professional service managers stems from their structural position within provider units. They are well positioned to become involved in the various cycles of activity; negotiating, for example, the case for changes with general managers who must agree and sanction additional resources, or exploring a question related to standards with representatives of the relevant professional body. They also provide a link between the different interests in quality across the health service. As practitioners themselves, they can appreciate the technical concerns of the professional service providers. As managers they are concerned with the generic issues related to how their service operates. And they are able to provide the links between their particular service and its integration into broader and more comprehensive service packages at the directorate or departmental level and at the level of the hospital or community service unit, that concern general managers and purchasers. Without such links, there is a danger that audit programmes become increasingly divorced from the main business of the organization.

Hitherto, the involvement of general management in clinical audit could be characterized as conspicuous by its absence! This is partly explained by other, more pressing demands[14] and partly by the desire to encourage the development of audit by leaving the feeling of 'ownership' with the professionals concerned. But general management has been increasingly involved in auditing general standards, as laid down in the Health of the Nation[15] and the Patients Charter[16]. This illustrates the concern of general management with the broader generic and systemic quality issues, such as patient satisfaction and the fulfilment of service contracts. General managers are also increasingly involved in the promotion of other quality assurance initiatives. It makes sense if these can be combined with audit rather than competing with it for time and commitment.

The study also suggests that by virtue of their position and authority within organizational structures, general managers are able to assist in progressing the audit cycle, particularly in enabling change to occur, and have considerable potential for developing multi-professional audit. This latter attribute is considered further in the final section of the paper.

The evidence from the study indicated that purchasers were similar to general managers in not having been much involved with audit, hitherto, and the little involvement they had experienced had been of a general nature. But this was seen as changing; audit monies were going to be disbursed by purchasers and audit was going to play a larger part in the contracting process. Purchasers are concerned with the technical quality of care, as applied to patients for whom they purchase treatment and care, as well as with the broader generic and systemic aspects of quality. In satisfying the former concern they may bypass general managers in the provider units and create links directly with professional service managers and practitioners.

Purchasers have a choice as to how far they wish to directly monitor quality, perhaps undertaking their own reviews, as opposed to commissioning a review by a third party or, as appears most common, requiring that the service providers are, themselves, adequately monitoring quality[17]. The latter course means that at a minimum purchasers will be concerned that audit arrangements are in place, and that they have some sight of the results. This raises problems of confidentiality and the communication of sensitive information between different market interests. It also poses a problem in that the interests of the purchasers in commissioning audit may not be the same as the professional practitioners who are going to carry it out. Whereas it might be expected that purchasers would be concerned with outcomes and quality of care for their patients and with the use of resources, it has already been suggested that the professional practitioners are likely to emphasize the technical processes of care, and their managers how that care is managed. Further, audit also serves an important function in professional training and development that will be of immediate concern to the practitioners and their managers. The Department of Health recognized the possibility of such conflicts of purpose in its advice on new arrangements for purchasing audit, suggesting that recognition be given to the priorities of both purchasers and providers when negotiating audit contracts[6].

Given the different levels of involvement with audit across the health service, and the different interests in what it should examine, there is a case for providing organizational structures that enable linkages to occur and different interests to be clarified and negotiated. This is not possible if the linkage is primarily dependent upon the transmission of aggregated reports.

1. The professional service practitioners and their managers readily came together, both within the audit process itself and through regular staff meetings. Where the audit process only involved small groups of the staff, as was often the case, staff meetings commonly included an 'audit item' to enable a wider report.

2. There were also unit audit or quality committees. In theory these integrated the audit activities of different disciplines and enabled general managers to make an input into the process. In reality their status appeared unclear; in some cases they were really dealing with medical audit, in others with everything but; in some cases they were concerned with developing 'top-down' quality assurance initiatives, in others they were attempting to co-ordinate all quality related activities, including audit. The authority of these committees *vis à vis* the disciplines undertaking audit was frequently unclear and they did not necessarily incorporate members who could commit their disciplines to undertake audit or explain the work that had been done. In its advice on the future development of clinical audit, the Department of Health suggested that organizations co-ordinated all their audit activities by creating a Clinical Audit Co-ordinating Group or Committee that incorporated both clinical staff and managers, under a chairperson who reported directly to the Trust Board. Although such a body would provide for co-ordination at the unit level, it might be beneficial to:

    • provide for a similar body at the sub-unit or directorate, since this level also requires service integration and co-ordination, chaired by, or responsible to, the Clinical Director or Patient Services Manager;

    • make arrangements for some members of the Unit Clinical Audit Co-ordinating Group or Committee to meet regularly with purchasing managers in a District or Purchasing Agency Audit Co-ordinating Committee, to negotiate purchaser and provider interests in audit. The Department of Health has already suggested that the Chair of the Unit Clinical Audit Committee should be involved in the contract negotiating process[6].

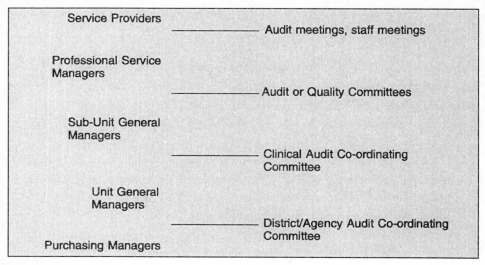

Figure 3

Mechanisms for integrating clinical audit

The suggested structures to co-ordinate and develop audit activities are set out in Figure 3. The mechanisms also help to draw audit activities into the main-stream business of the health service, which is a further Departmental objective.

Multi-professional audit

To return to the starting point and the research brief, what was the potential for multi-professional audit?

On the evidence from the study there was markedly less engagement with multi-professional audit activities than with uni-professional (46 as opposed to 89 audits in the six main fieldwork sites). The reasons given were: evolutionary, that you master what you know best before moving to less familiar ground; organizational, that multi-professional audit lacked the clear hierarchical accountability to the service professional manager that existed for uni-professional audit; and methodological, that multi-professional audit lacked clear and agreed standards of assessment. To quote one of the respondents in the study, 'Multi-professional audit is only as good as uni-professional standards'.

Multi-professional audit has considerable strengths, directing attention to patients' needs rather than the needs of staff disciplines, and avoiding duplication of effort and waste of resources. The institutions providing hospital and community care have, with the introduction of devolved resource management, increasingly organized their activities around the output of patient services—surgery, care of the elderly—rather than around the inputs provided by staff disciplines[18]. Service contracts, too, are increasingly framed in the same way. So it makes sense for audit activities to reflect multi-disciplinary objectives.

The study suggests that:

- you need strong uni-professional audit to move into multi-professional audit activities;

- multi-professional audit requires sponsorship by general managers and purchasers. Given that non-medical audit appears to be largely initiated and led hierarchically, it is the general managers who are in a position to bring the different non-medical disciplines together and direct engagement in multi-professional audit. Purchasers can have the same effect through the contractual process;

- structures can be devised to facilitate both audit in general and multi-professional audit. Proposals have been set out in Figure 3 above;

- multi-professional audit will entail an increased emphasis on generic and systemic quality concerns and less concentration on technical issues concerned with treatment and care processes. This may serve to bring clinical audit closer to other forms of quality initiative.

Finally, it should be borne in mind that if clinical audit is to be thought of as a generic activity, it is likely to benefit from the strength of all its species, whether these are uni or multi-professional in their form.

Acknowledgments

The research reported in this paper was undertaken by a team jointly directed by Professor Maurice Kogan, of the Centre for Evaluation of Public Policy and Practice, Brunel University, and Professor Sally Redfern, of the Nursing Research Unit, Kings College, London. Other members of the team included, in addition to the author, Dr Anemone Kober, who undertook much of the fieldwork, Dr Ian Norman and Ms Sarah Robinson. The findings and analyses discussed in the paper are the result of co-operative work by the team; their interpretation is the responsibility of the author. The paper should in no way be seen as representing the views of the Department of Health.

The research report *Clinical Audit in Four Health Professions* was presented to the Department of Health in 1994. The material is also to be shortly published as a book, *Making Use of*

Clinical Audit: A Guide to Practice in the Health Professions, by M Kogan and S Redfern, with A Kober, I Norman, T Packwood and S Robinson, Open University Press, 1995.

References

1   Secretaries of State for Health. *Working for Patients* (Cmd 55). London: HMSO, 1989

2   Ellis R, Whittington D. *Quality assurance in healthcare: a handbook*. London: Edward Arnold, 1993

3   Department of Health. *Clinical audit: meeting and improving standards in healthcare*. London: Department of Health, 1993

4   Department of Health. *Clinical audit in the nursing and therapy professions*. London: Department of Health, 1994

5   Normand C, Ditch J, Dockrell J, *et al. Clinical audit in professions allied to medicine and related therapy professions*. Belfast: Health and Health Care Research Unit, Queens University, Belfast, 1991

6   Department of Health, EL(94)20. *Clinical audit: 1994/95 and beyond*. London: Department of Health, 1994

7   Department of Health. *The evolution of clinical audit*. London: Department of Health, 1994

8   Donabedian A. Quality assessment and assurance. *Inquiry* 1988; **25**: 173–92

9   Shaw C. *Medical audit: a hospital handbook*. London: Kings Fund Centre, 1990

10   Crombie I, Davies H. The missing link in the audit cycle. *Qual Health Care* 1993; **12**: 47–8

11   Kerrison S, Packwood T, Buxton M. *Medical audit: taking stock*. London: Kings Fund Centre, 1993

12   Joss R, Henkel M, Kogan M. *Total Quality Management in the National Health Service: final report of an evaluation*. Uxbridge: CEPP, Brunel University, 1994

13   Packwood T, Kerrison S, Buxton M. The audit process and medical organisation. *Qual Health Care* 1992; **1**:192–6

14   Buttery Y, Walshe K, Coles J, Bennett J. *Evaluating audit: the development of audit*. London: CASPE, 1994

15   Department of Health. *Health of the Nation: a consultative document for health in England*. London: HMSO, 1991

16   Department of Health. *The Patients' Charter*. London: HMSO, 1991

17   Ovretveit J. *Purchasing for health*. Buckingham: Open University Press, 1995

18   Packwood T, Keen J, Buxton M. Process and structure: resource management and the development of sub-unit organisational structure. *Health Services Manage Res* 1992; **5**: 66–76

Are purchasers ready for clinical audit?

JOANNE LORD AND PETER LITTLEJOHNS

HEALTH CARE EVALUATION UNIT, ST GEORGE'S HOSPITAL MEDICAL SCHOOL, LONDON, UK

In 1989 a programme of clinical audit was introduced throughout the UK NHS in an attempt to improve care through the application of quality methodologies to clinical issues. There were many motivations and influences behind this national initiative, and this is reflected in the plurality of organizational and methodological approaches that have been taken to clinical audit in this country[1]. The Department of Health publication *The A-Z of Quality*[2] lists over 300 projects (selected from over 2500) involving many professional groups and organizations and utilizing a wide range of quality methods, from accreditation to Total Quality Management. Clinical audit is just one strand within this complex quality picture.

The evolution of clinical audit policy

Donabedian has described the US health care quality movement as exhibiting 'unity of purpose, diversity of means'[3]. Is this also the case in the UK? Whilst there is general agreement that the ultimate purpose of clinical audit is to improve patient outcomes, it is less clear how this is to be achieved. Various mechanisms through which audit might work have been put forward[4]. It might work directly by bringing about immediate changes in clinician behaviour. Or, if it creates a supportive environment promoting personal or team development, it may improve clinical practice in the longer term. If inefficiencies are identified through audit, resources may be released for use elsewhere. Or information from audit may be used to inform purchasing decisions (between competing interventions and/or

EVALUATING CLINICAL AUDIT: PAST LESSONS, FUTURE DIRECTIONS, EDITED BY KIERAN WALSHE, 1995.
INTERNATIONAL CONGRESS AND SYMPOSIUM SERIES NO 212 PUBLISHED BY ROYAL SOCIETY OF MEDICINE PRESS LIMITED

between competing providers) leading to health gain through shifts in contracts or greater pressure on contracted providers to improve. These mechanisms have different implications for the organization and conduct of clinical audit. A much greater level of purchaser involvement is indicated if gains from audit are thought to accrue largely through the latter mechanisms. Uncertainty and disagreement over the relative importance of these various mechanisms is a major cause of uncertainty over the appropriate role of purchasers in clinical audit[5].

The 'fundamental principles' of medical audit set out in the 1989 working paper[6] place great emphasis on the need for professional ownership of the initiative, recognizing only a peripheral role for management in agreeing the arrangements for audit with the local committee. Management were also to have access to 'general results' of audit and the right to initiate independent audits when necessary. Medical audit was seen as a potential source of information for purchasers, but in terms of the general arrangements not specific findings:

'Audit arrangements are one of the factors health authorities will wish to take into account when taking decisions about the allocation of contracts . . .'[6]

Initial financial mechanisms to support audit reinforced professional dominance: medical audit, and to a much lesser degree nursing and therapy audit, were developed in a protected environment outside the NHS internal market (see Figure 1).

With the cessation of ringfenced funding for clinical audit in the hospital and community health services from April 1994, regions were asked to promote the use of clinical audit as part of the purchasers role in contracting[7]. Attached to this executive letter was a paper by a working group of the Regional Medical Audit Coordinators and the Conference of Royal Colleges' Audit Group. This proposed a more active role for purchasers, including negotiation over the choice of audit topics. In return there was to be a greater role for clinicians in negotiations relating to clinical audit and quality specifications in contracts. The call for an enhanced role for purchasers and the embedding of audit within the contracting system was reiterated in the policy statements *Meeting and improving standards in health care*[8] and *The evolution of clinical audit*[9] (see Figure 2). The nature of contracting mechanisms for clinical audit are discussed further in the recent letter from the Department of Health[10].

Clinical audit, involving all the health professions, should be a major plank in the complete quality assurance that purchasers require of the units with which they place contracts... Of course, purchasers must recognize that some aspects of audit are best carried out in complete confidence by the professions concerned. But they must be

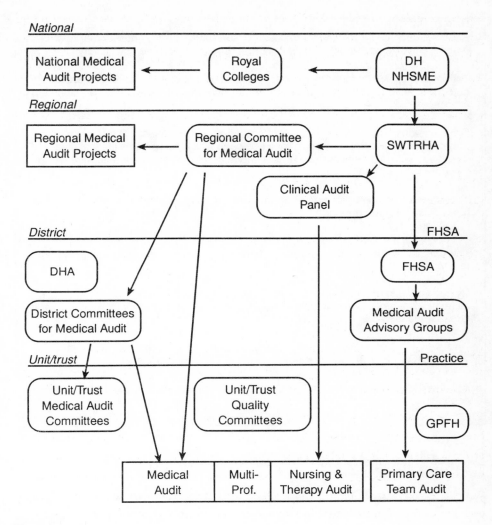

Figure 1

Flow of funds for clinical audit 1990–94

assured that appropriate action is being taken in response to audit findings and that improvements are being achieved. And they should not be afraid if necessary to use the contracting process to make sure that this happens[11].

This shift in emphasis on the respective roles of healthcare professionals, provider managers and purchasers begs the question 'are purchasers ready for audit?' In responding to this question it is important to identify the extent to which audit programmes developed over the

Audit will become largely multi-professional and part of a wider quality management programme that spans all aspects of care in hospitals and the community.

The management contribution to clinical audit will be enhanced. Generation of outcome data will be of little value unless that can be integrated into management processes.

Clinical audit must remain clinically led and educationally based. The move to multi-professional working should take place at a pace which participants at local level find consistent with the development and acceptance of uni-professional standards and values.

The practice of audit remains a professional activity. Purchasers of health care, health service managers and patients however will increasingly influence the audit programme.

The general results of clinical audit will increasingly inform service development and contracting.

By continuing to prove its effectiveness, audit will become part of routine practice for all healthcare professionals and a normal expectation of those who commission and finance health care.

Understanding of the effectiveness of interventions will improve with increasing sophistication of outcome measurement and information systems.

Audit will become an integral part of basic, undergraduate, postgraduate and continuing education.

Figure 2

Longer terms goals for clinical audit, from meeting and improving standards in healthcare[8]

past four or five years have linked to the contracting and health service management systems. Have purchasers been involved in the establishment and development of audit programmes? Have they helped to set the local audit agenda, to conduct audit or to implement the findings of audit? What are the perceptions of the various parties about the success or otherwise of any such links, and what are their attitudes towards the future development of closer links in line with DH guidance?

As part of a three-year research programme investigating the relationships between clinical audit and contracting, we collected information on existing levels of purchaser involvement, and on attitudes towards this involvement. The programme of work is summarized below. We then consider theoretical models of the purchaser role in clinical audit proposed in the literature and suggest a constructive but manageable way forward.

Study methods

First, we scanned the published and 'grey' literature, conferences and informal contacts to identify the extent of the issues involved. This evidence is reviewed in our interim report[12]. In order to observe existing relationships and attitudes in South West Thames, information was collected from a range of sources:

- A series of regional workshops consisting of professionals, purchasers and provider managers was held to discuss the issues and explore differing perspectives.

- A systematic review of clinical audit annual reports was conducted to identify formal arrangements and stated intentions.

- Semi-structured interviews were undertaken with the chairs of medical audit committees to assess their perceptions and attitudes.

- Purchasing intentions for a sample of Authorities in South West Thames were reviewed to assess their stated expectations of audit programmes and quality specifications in general.

Each of these investigations is described in more detail below. Following these qualitative studies, a postal attitude survey of healthcare professionals and managers is now being conducted in three local Trusts, with different styles of clinical audit programme. The results of this survey will be available later this year.

Following the report *Medical Audit and the Manager*[13] the NHS Training Directorate promoted discussions in the regions over the appropriate role for purchasers and provider managers in audit. In South West Thames a working group was convened to address the issues. The report of this group presented checklists of the responsibilities of provider managers and purchasers towards audit and *vice versa*[14]. Following this report, two workshops were held in January and February 1993 to discuss the issues further. Sixty-five local health care professionals and managers from purchasing and providing organizations attended these events[15].

Medical audit committees (both district and unit based for the hospital and community health services and Medical Audit Advisory Groups for the family health services) have been required to produce annual reports by the Department of Health since 1990. These are public documents that provided accountability for audit funds, reported on progress, and set out the expressed intentions of the committees who ran medical audit at a local level.

In an analysis of 28 annual audit reports for 1990/91 and 1991/92 from South West Thames, Dr Ronnie Ooi compared their content with criteria set out in national and regional policy statements[16]. Five central and five regional policy circulars were examined, and 72 separate criteria for the content of annual reports were identified. The criteria covered the organization, staffing and finance of audit programmes along with activities, results and future strategy, and included requirements to state the nature and extent of links with purchasers and provider management.

As part of a purchaser development project with Mid Surrey Health Authority[17], a series of interviews was conducted with the chairs of medical audit committees in the old South West Thames Region[12]. The interviews took place between December 1992 and April 1993. Ten of the 14 hospital and community committees and two of the five MAAGs were covered. A proforma was used to structure the interviews, which lasted between half an hour and two hours. Questions covered perceptions and opinions about local relationships between various professional groups organizing and conducting clinical audit and between these groups and purchasers and provider managers. The level of involvement non-clinicians at various stages of the audit cycle was assessed and examples of collaboration were solicited.

Each Autumn District Health Authorities and General Practitioner fundholders publish their purchasing intentions to inform the forthcoming contracting round. The documents incorporate feedback from local consultations with providers, GPs and the public, and set out goals and concerns over the mix and quality of services, as well as expected resource constraints, population needs/demands and purchasing priorities.

1994/95 purchasing intention documents were reviewed for six out of the, then, 10 DHAs in South West Thames[12]. Statements referring to quality requirements or quality assurance processes (including clinical audit) were extracted and classified in three ways: by the service/ speciality area to which they applied; by the aspect of quality addressed (using Maxwell's dimensions of healthcare quality and Donabedian's Structure-Process-Outcome taxonomy[18,19]); and by the nature of the specification, ie. whether it set a standard, a guideline or a quality process to be used by providers (see Figure 3).

The intention of this review was to assess, subjectively but systematically, the degree and spread of purchaser interest in quality assurance and improvement across the region as expressed through the medium of purchasing intentions documents. Though, of course, the number of 'quality statements' can only be a crude indicator of the importance placed by purchasers on the various aspects of quality.

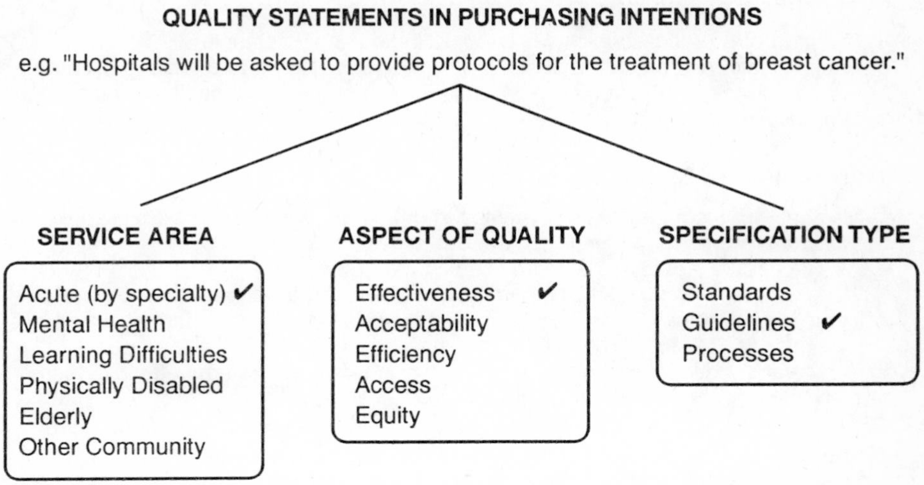

QUALITY STATEMENTS IN PURCHASING INTENTIONS

e.g. "Hospitals will be asked to provide protocols for the treatment of breast cancer."

SERVICE AREA

Acute (by specialty) ✔
Mental Health
Learning Difficulties
Physically Disabled
Elderly
Other Community

ASPECT OF QUALITY

Effectiveness   ✔
Acceptability
Efficiency
Access
Equity

SPECIFICATION TYPE

Standards
Guidelines   ✔
Processes

Figure 3
Classification of quality statements in purchasing intentions documents

Findings from regional workshops

These events highlighted the disparate views across the region, not only between but also within the 'three tribes' of audit (provider management, provider clinicians and purchasers). In particular, there was disagreement over the feasibility and desirability of using information from audit to inform purchasing or management decisions. Some clinicians, along with some purchasers, felt very strongly that this would not be compatible with the function of audit as a professionally owned, educational device. Others felt that audit could fulfil both functions, and that without external scrutiny clinical audit would remain unchallenging and sterile (failing to tackle real problems and 'bad apples').

The practical difficulties of purchasers taking a more active role in audit were also highlighted. Participants emphasized the constraints on purchasers' time and expertise, and the technical problems of allowing for case-mix when using audit information in a comparative manner. At the second workshop Diana Forrest reported the findings of a quick telephone survey of 12 public health physicians from 12 out of the 13 districts in the region. Their comments reinforced the lack of consensus demonstrated at the workshops (see Figure 4).

Interviews with medical audit chairpersons

The chairs of the medical audit committees reported low levels of involvement from purchasers, who were seen as taking a 'hands off' approach. There was very little 'active' involvement

Positive

- The start of a process which will become increasingly valuable
- Public Health can provide a useful link. It is unthreatening to clinicians. Can help with methodology. Are familiar with sources of data. Can be objective. Understand purchasers' point of view.

Equivocal

- Medical Audit is important but yet little information. Must be owned by clinicians.
- MA and management should be 'hand in glove'
- All purchasers would like to influence what is audited
- They can suggest topics but these may not be of great interest to clinicians
- Their influence may be through provider management rather than via the Audit Committee
- They want audit that demonstrates a better understanding of the effectiveness of care, linking GP, hospital & community services

Negative

- Problems with audit: Lack of energy to implement change
- Some clinicians need reminding of what audit is
- No mention of anything happening as a result of the involvement of District or Unit General Manager
- Feedback to purchasers (divided opinions). Information from clinicians is of no value for purchasers.
- 'Medical Audit is the biggest tragedy of missed opportunity'
- 'We are doing it in a way which would make most business managers laugh'

Figure 4

Telephone survey of 12 public health physicians in South West Thames in January 1993

(selecting topics, taking decisions over use of funds and involvement in making changes as a result of audit) of either purchasers or provider managers. Only a handful of examples were cited where purchasers had initiated audits. The level of 'passive' involvement (knowledge of topics, receipt of aggregated results) was also low. The main link between purchasers and the local medical audit committees was through the Director of Public Health (usually a member of the committee, but not always active). Attitudes towards greater purchaser and management involvement with audit varied greatly: some welcomed it and felt that there were good relationships in their locality and a genuine desire to cooperate; others accepted it as inevitable but had reservations; and some feared that information would be misused to penalize poor performers or to take decisions on the basis of cost rather than quality (see Figure 5).

Review of medical audit committee annual reports

The review of medical audit annual reports suggested that there was uneven communication and coordination between audit committees and purchaser/provider management. Many

---

Should provider managers be more involved/informed of audit activity?

No difficulty. Likely to happen in future.

Yes—and they will be, but it will not be easy. A small number of consultants are unhappy about sharing information with managers. We can overcome this by more open discussion.

No need to rock the boat. More involvement could be a potential problem, as management wearing a different hat could lead to a conflict of interests. Need to distinguish audit on medical issues (which need to remain with doctors for free and open discussion amongst them) and audit on service issues (in which management do have a legitimate interest).

Not very high priority. Initially concerned to keep clinicians enthusiasm, for which confidentiality is necessary.

Double edged sword—only looking for ways to cheaper healthcare, may cut corners. Communication is alright—they should get reports, but not be too closely involved.

Should purchasers be more involved/informed of audit activity?

Yes, more involvement. If there is to be more 'clinical audit', we will need to integrate everyone in the process (purchasers, providers, the community and GPs— especially as purchasers).

It is healthy to have purchasers on DCMA. Against them setting the agenda—audit is for professionals. Medical audit was not set up to be used as a 'stick' or 'controlling instrument', and if it is it will discredit audit with clinicians. The appropriate forum for discussion is at a directorate level with the local director of quality.

Legitimate right in principle. But there is muted opposition because of a lack of trust. Purchasers have not been forthcoming, they are doing their own audit and trying to get the audit funds.

Provider management has more right than purchaser—audit has implications for effectiveness. Worry is purchaser could tell us what to do, eg guidelines (HotN).

Concerned that it would be commercially related, not a long-term view but 'number crunching'.

Figure 5

Interviews with chairs of audit committees in South West Thames in 1992/3

committees did express a belief that better links should be built between the professionally-run committees, Trust management and the Health Authorities, or announced that they intended to improve these links, but few reported positive initiatives in these areas.

For example, nine of the 13 committees for whom 1990/91 reports were available reported that they intended to build links between the clinical audit programme and contracting/

Table 1   *Content of 1990/91 medical audit reports and reported changes in 1991/92 reports for 13 district medical audit committees in South West Thames*

Criteria	1990/91 Yes	1990/91 Planned	Implemented	Still planned	Not mentioned	Dropped	NA
Link with district information officer	5	1					1
Link with resource management	2	6	1	3	1	1	
Link with QA director/ programmes	1	6		1	4		1
Link with contracting (purchasing)		9		3	3	1	2
District and unit general managers involved		7		1	4		2
Managers to receive regular reports	1	2			2		

(Column group heading: *Changes reported in 91/92 for those in planned category for in 90/91* spans Implemented, Still planned, Not mentioned, Dropped, NA)

Notes: "yes" means criteria planned or implemented; "planned" means criterion supported and/or implementation planned; left blank means criterion not mentioned. Reports for 1990/91 were available from 13 district medical audit committees in South West Thames

purchasing (none said that they had already done so). Of these nine, none stated in their 1991/92 report that they had actually implemented this intention: three merely repeated the intention; three did not mention it at all; one said they had dropped the intention; and 1992/93 reports were not available for the other two committees (see Table 1).

Review of purchasing intentions

Analysis of the content of purchasing intentions documents reveals a long list of quality indicators being used by purchasers, many of which reflect national and regional priority areas. Not surprisingly, the documents contained many statements related to the *acceptability* of services to patients (provision of user/carer information, advice and support . . .) or to patient *access* to services (waiting times for inpatient and outpatient appointments . . .). These were derived mainly from the Patient's Charter, Community Care and Health of the Nation white papers and policy guidance. Rather more surprisingly, there were also a large number of statements relating to the clinical *effectiveness* of services, mainly derived from the Health of the

Nation First Steps recommendations and from local health strategy work, with some Community Care issues. The purchasers also emphasized the need for *efficiency*, in terms of Cost Improvement Programmes, targets for length of stay, day case surgery and outpatient follow-up rates. However, the number of *equity* statements was very low, two of the six Health Authorities in the sample did not have a single statement in their purchasing intentions document relating to the fair treatment of users or staff from different racial, ethnic, gender or age groups by contracted providers.

Statements related to quality standards, guidelines or processes and varied in strength— sometimes purchasers explicitly quoted given standards or guidelines that they expected/ required contracted providers of given services to meet:

'Thrombolysis after MI: >50% to receive streptokinase and aspirin on arrival. Door to needle time: >80% to be treated within 30 mins.'

In other cases, purchasers stated that they expected/required standards or guidelines to be agreed during contract negotiations:

'Before contracting with any provider for ENT services [the DHA] will expect to see a detailed protocol for the Unit setting out thresholds for surgical intervention and care regimes for 'glue ear' and T&A's ... .'

Or sometimes they stated that standards/guidelines should be developed over a longer timescale:

'The Authority will encourage the development of local guidelines for good practice in the management of [asthma], including the role of the protocol for shared care between the Consultants [in 2 local providers] and the local General Practitioners and criteria for hospital admission.'

Similarly statements relating to quality processes were more or less specific over the methodology to be used, and over the method of implementation:

'All providers who provide acute or rehabilitation care for patients with cerebrovascular disease will be asked to undertake at least one clinical audit of an aspect of their service and to make the summary results of this audit available to the purchaser.'

All Authorities made some reference to their expectations of providers' clinical audit arrangements or requested audits on given topics:

'... review of the use of arthroscopy should be included with the medical audit programme.'

'Providers of acute care for ... asthma patients will be asked to undertake at least one clinical audit ... preferably addressing the interface between primary and secondary care and which pays specific attention to outcome measures. Summary results ... should be made available to the purchaser.'

'The Authority will continue to focus on specific protocols for medical and nursing interventions. A clear audit programme will be required at the beginning of the contractual process and this will be seen as an integral part of the providers' business plan. The Authority will specify protocols/packages of care in terms of overall improvement in the health of individuals, paying particular attention to the Health of the Nation ...'

Of course, the number of quality statements in purchaser documents may be a poor guide to their real priorities and activity. The purchasing intentions documents represent a pre-negotiation stance and, without clear definitions and agreement between purchasers and providers (including clinicians) on responsibilities for implementation and monitoring, many statements will not be credible. The documents studied frequently failed to indicate whether these conditions had been met, or whether they were to be addressed in contract negotiations. As might be expected, most specifications related to the structure or process of health care, not directly to outcome, and some statements were very weak:

'Patients to be given adequate knowledge about the drugs prescribed to them, including side effects.'

'Providers will be asked to ensure that service users are involved in the planning, monitoring and development of local services.'

It is easy to be suspicious that many of these words will not be followed up with action. Often clinicians are not aware of contract specifications relating to their work and are not involved in their negotiation. Without their participation many quality improvements are not deliverable. Nevertheless, the analysis of Purchasing Intentions does show a high level of interest from purchasers in the quality of the services that they commission, including, in some cases, quite detailed interest in aspects of clinical care.

Models of interaction

The literature on clinical audit is extensive, and much of it touches on the role of purchasers within audit. Commentators have suggested many different models of the audit/contracting relationship, with differing roles for purchasers. Using the language of 'Soft Systems Methodology'[20,21] to articulate these models, we have identified four (of the many possible) models[22]:

1. **Isolationist** eg[23]

    This proposes a view of audit as a professionally owned, peer-review or self-review activity, organized through professional associations and/or local professional committees. It's primary aim is quality improvement through professional development and the transfer of knowledge and skills. Hence confidentiality within the profession is of prime importance, and the role of purchasers and provider managers is minimal, basically limited to the provision of resources to support audit. Largely uni-disciplinary, professions and specialities could choose to cooperate.

2. **Intermediate** eg[24]

    The model proposed within Working Paper 6 went somewhat beyond this. It emphasized the importance of professional ownership, but extended the role of non-clinicians to the one of oversight, monitoring, strategic involvement and independent action (under exceptional circumstances).

3. **Integrated** eg[25]

    Under an integrated model, clinical audit would be seen as part of organizational quality assurance for providers and/or purchasers. Much more open access to the results of audits would be necessary, providing a source of information to guide managerial and purchasing decisions. Audit would be integral to contracting, performing a major role in defining and monitoring clinical quality.

4. **Split**

    Lying some way between the isolationist and integrated models, a split model of audit would differ from the intermediate model in making an explicit distinction between two types of audit. Clinicians would retain 'protected space' for self and peer review, to allow them to pursue their own interests and tackle difficult issues in a supportive, educational environment. At the same time a manageable programme of shared audits would be developed between clinicians, provider management and purchasers, to address priority issues and encourage a more open approach.

The 'split' system of audit has similarities with that proposed by for Scotland, with the Area Clinical Audit Committees responsible for the coordination of shared audits[26]. It has also been proposed for use in primary health care, with a 'two-track' programme of internal and external audits[27]. This idea represents a 'mixed-scanning' approach to audit, seeking to balance the rationalistic goals of a 'top-down' approach with the more realistic, and sensitive goals of an incrementalist approach[28].

Conclusions

The findings of this review suggest that there has been little active involvement of purchasers in the development of clinical audit systems or in deciding the content of audit programmes. There are examples of purchaser initiatives in these areas, but these are relatively rare, and of limited scope. Examples of purchaser action as a result of clinical audit findings (shifting contracts or adding quality specifications) are even rarer. The major route of influence on clinical audit for purchasers has been through the participation of Public Health representatives on audit committees. In terms of monitoring audit activity, most purchasers do little more than examine audit committee annual reports or minutes (which usually contain few results).

Despite the difficulties, purchasers are increasingly expressing a desire to 'get their hands dirty', becoming more involved in issues of clinical effectiveness. They are making a large number of quality specifications, in many cases very detailed prescriptive specifications relating to clinical aspects of care not just 'hotel' issues. Though much of this may be rhetoric, some purchasers are beginning to attach incentives or disincentives to specifications, for instance 'buying' audits from providers on particular topics. The number of quality specifications does present a logistic and managerial problem for many providers, and a more targeted approach to quality improvement may actually be much more productive. However, it is difficult for authorities, given the necessity of responding to the large number of central initiatives.

The shift in funding from region to local purchasers has had some impact. On average, DHAs in the western half of South Thames received £240 000 for clinical audit in 1994/5. Though this is only a very small proportion (0.2%) of their total revenue budgets, it is seen as providing some scope for pump-priming new initiatives in priority areas. Negotiations over audit contracts have including specific requirements for audit activity, although less powerful, or less interested, purchasers have simply continued to hand over audit money to providers according to historical funding patterns, attaching few conditions on its use.

So, overall purchasers have not chosen to, or have not felt able to, use clinical audit as a lever for change or as a source of information on clinical effectiveness. In some cases this may be an active decision that this is not an appropriate purchaser role, and would be too threatening, undermining the growth and educational potential of audit. In many other cases purchasers are simply not ready for audit, they have too many other more pressing priorities demanding attention. Given these conditions, a constructive way forward for purchasers is to maintain existing professionally-led and provider-led clinical audit programmes, ensuring that an active and comprehensive programme is underway, and to develop a small number of collaborative audit projects together with providers on issues of particular interest.

References

1   Shaw CD. Quality assurance in the United Kingdom. *Qual Health Care* 1993; **5**: 107–18

2   Department of Health. *The A–Z of quality: a guide to quality initiatives in the NHS.* Leeds: NHSME, 1993

3   Donabedian A. Quality assessment and assurance: unity of purpose, diversity of means. *Inquiry* 1988; Spring: 90–9

4   Lord J, Littlejohns P. Clinical audit: secret garden. *Health Serv J* 1994; **104**: 18–20

5   Ovretveit J. Purchasing for health gain: the problems and prospects for purchasing for health gain in the 'managed markets' of the NHS and other European health systems. *Eur J Public Health* 1993; **3**: 77–84

6   Department of Health. *Medical audit. NHS review working paper 6.* London: HMSO, 1989

7   Department of Health. EL(93)34. *Clinical audit in HCHS: allocation of funds 1993/94.* London: Department of Health, 1993

8   Department of Health. EL(93)59. *Clinical audit: meeting and improving standards in healthcare.* London: Department of Health, 1993

9   Department of Health. *The evolution of clinical audit.* London: Department of Health, 1994

10   Department of Health. EL(94)20. *Clinical audit: 1994/95 and beyond.* London: Department of Health, 1994

11   Department of Health. Purchasing for health: a framework for action. Speeches by Dr Brian Mawhinney MP and Sir Duncan Nichol 1993

12   Lord J, Littlejohns P. *Clinical audit, contracting and effectiveness: interim report.* London: Health Care Evaluation Unit, St George's Hospital Medical School, 1994

13   Harman D, Martin G. *Medical audit and the manager: a discussion document.* Birmingham: Health Services Management Centre, University of Birmingham, 1991

14   Littlejohns P. *Medical audit and management. A discussion paper for doctors and managers.* London: Health Care Evaluation Unit, St George's Hospital Medical School, 1992

15   Cluzeau F. *Realising the benefits of medical audit: the role of purchasers and providers.* London: Health Care Evaluation Unit, St George's Hospital Medical School, 1993

16 Ooi ROS. *Audit of the annual reports of audit committees in South West Thames region.* London: South West Thames RHA, 1993

17 Pharoah C, Durman L. *A purchaser review: current guidance and evidence on clinical standards for ENT services.* London: South West Thames RHA, 1993

18 Maxwell RJ. Dimensions of quality revisited: from thought to action. *Qual Health Care* 1992; **1**: 171–7

19 Hopkins A, Maxwell RJ. Contracts and quality of care. *BMJ* 1990; **300**: 919–22

20 Checkland P, Scholes J. Soft systems methodology in action. Chichester: John Wiley & Sons, 1990

21 Gains A, Rosenhead J. *Problem structuring for medical quality assurance.* Working paper series in Operational Research, 1993

22 Lord J, Littlejohns P. Links between clinical audit and contracting systems. *Int J Health Care Qual Assur* 1995; 8

23 Royal College of Physicians. *Medical audit: a first report. What, why and how?* London: Royal College of Physicians, 1989

24 Macpherson D, Mann T. Medical audit and quality of care—a new English initiative. *Qual Assur Health Care* 1992; **4**: 89–95

25 Spiers J. *From medical mystery to public rationality: scrutiny, individual responsibility & the secret garden. The NHS League Tables as public documents and tools for change.* 1994

26 Scottish Office. *The interface between clinical audit and management.* A report of a Working Group set up by the Clinical Resource and Audit Group. Chairman Sir Thomas J Thomson, 1993

27 Metcalf DHH. Audit in general practice: two track programme needed. *BMJ* 1989; **299**: 1293–4

28 Etzioni A. Mixed scanning: a 'third' approach to decision making. In: Faludi A, ed. *A reader in planning theory.* Oxford: Pergamon Press, 1973